MAINTAIN YOUR GEAR

MAINTAIN YOUR GEAR

SUREFIRE STRATEGIES TO DOMINATE, EXECUTE, AND SCALE IN BUSINESS AND LIFE

JOSEPH McCABE

Forefront
BOOKS

To my Pop, Charles K. McBrearty, thank you for being my hero and the embodiment of the person I aspire to be. I continue to work in your shadow, and I always will. You're the only unconditional friend I have ever had.

To my Pop, James McCabe, thank you for showing me that it's okay to work hard and define your own love and happiness, ignoring all others, even family. Thank you for showing me freedom.

To my mother and father, I haven't made it where I wanted to yet, but I will, and it's all because of the work ethic you taught me and your other four sons—a relentless drive for greatness. You have five successful sons, an accomplishment most could not achieve.

I have to thank my amazing, hard-working wife, Alexis McCabe. From reading and editing my early drafts to giving me advice on the cover, she was as important to this book getting done as I was. She did it all while working full time and wrapping up her Master as a Nurse practitioner. I would not have done it without her push! Thank you and I Love you!

CONTENTS

INTRODUCTION

Maintain your gear is a military saying that defines a way of life. It is the practice of owning everything in your world to an extreme degree. It means you are solely responsible for everything that has the potential to affect whether or not your mission is successful. This concept can be daunting at first but is ultimately empowering; once you accept that everything that happens does so because of you, you have the ultimate control. For example, one of the most common excuses for being late is traffic, but is that true? Was it the traffic itself, or did you not leave your last location with enough time to *allow* for traffic? No one cares that you're late because your alarm didn't go off; the world kept moving, and you missed out.

No matter if you're starting a company, growing a company, working in sales, or trying to reach goals that seem unattainable, you have to start by maintaining your gear. In the military, not having your magazines loaded, contact drills practiced, or personal fitness at top levels can lead to loss of life and even mass casualties. The team counts on you to maintain your gear at a baseline level so the unit can operate efficiently. All jobs are mission critical. No matter how seemingly small, they impact the overall outcome. The same principle of maintaining your gear can be applied in the foundation of all successful businesses.

My generation is completely fucked by the instant gratification and *carpe diem* mentality delivered by social media and well-meaning friends and family. The best tip I can give anyone is that if you would not trade places with the person giving you advice, don't take it. People don't realize this mentality is poison. I also would want to delay working and prioritize having fun if I knew that once I started working, I was guaranteed to be stuck with a car payment, a mortgage, and a nine-to-five existence for the next forty years and only a meager 401(k) to show for it. And that's if you're lucky. They call it the

"American Dream," but I call it the middle-class trap. However, you don't need to stay stuck in that trap if you're in it right now. You are equally responsible for *falling into* this trap as you are for *getting out* of it.

The first thing you have to do to get out of the trap is accept that you are in total control of both positive and negative outcomes. Next, identify your goals and everything standing in your way of accomplishing them. Want to lose weight? Cake and cookies are in your way. Everything standing in the way of your goals should be eliminated. Then make a list of everything you need to accomplish your goals and get to work. It's that simple.

If you are working toward a goal, the odds are stacked against you; 78 percent of small businesses fail in the first year.[1] Friends will get in your way, your family will try to pull you away, and ultimately time will become your enemy. So be prepared to make sacrifices and have conversations with yourself and those close to you to make sure that everyone is on the same page. Execution of the goal, whatever it is, is THE top priority. Anyone or anything not helping you advance toward your dreams is a hindrance. When done right, business is chaos; ensure that you thrive in it by maintaining stability in your home and personal life. Prioritize organization, routine, health, and relationships.

Chaos is created when action potential is maximized. In my everyday life, I ensure chaos by executing immediately. As soon as I get an idea, I write it down or text it to myself. Before I go to bed, I address everything I wrote down and then set my calendar for the next day. I always finish every task on my agenda. This technique of executing immediately on most ideas maximizes action potential and the likelihood of positive outcomes. Positive outcomes for me include partnerships, deals, cashflow, and ultimately freedom. I have more deals in the pipeline than I can count on two hands at any given time.

This is the chaos I thrive in and precisely why I emphasize calmness and order in my home life. There is no time to look for missing socks or clean sheets because I'm constantly executing. I create stability with an unwavering routine. I wake up at 7:30 a.m. every morning, go to Starbucks for a black iced coffee, and immediately get to work. After I have checked off all my tasks at the end of the day, I reward myself by hitting the gym and maintaining my health. I make time for my family in the evenings and on the weekends, and I vacation a few times a year. I work hard every day because I have created a system that works for me.

Maintaining your gear as a leader is crucial because it motivates the team and sets the standard. The leader's job is to ensure everyone has their gear before leaving for a mission. It is never the team's job to make sure you have what you need; as the leader, it's your job to have what you need so the team can function. Take full responsibility and ownership of life and anything that has the potential to affect it.

The only thing I have to sell to you is success.

This book is for leaders, salespeople, employees, students, soldiers, and anyone who wants to own their shit. If you can't figure out what is holding you back, this book will help you realize that *you* are holding *yourself* back. There are no secrets, gimmicks, or tricks in this book, nor is there a hidden agenda. The only thing I have to sell to you is success.

Fair warning, though: I don't believe in work-life balance. You will have to be ready to prioritize winning over balance, hard work over rest, and most importantly, yourself over the bullshit excuses you've been fed your whole life.

**Everything you want to achieve
needs to be earned . . . no
one owes you anything.**

In this book, you will understand that everything you want to achieve needs to be earned and that no one owes you anything. You will learn that the American Dream, middle-class mindset is the wrong target and is, in fact, a trap. In sales, *no* never means *no*; it just creates an opportunity for another point of contact. There is no shortage of money; you either don't know where to find the money, haven't discovered how to sell, or your pipeline isn't big enough. You will learn that customer acquisition is paramount to customer service and that, of course, the *best-known* product will always beat the *best* product on the market. The best tip I can give anyone is that if you would not trade places with the person giving you advice, don't take it.

WHO AM I?

I'm an entrepreneur from Philadelphia, Pennsylvania, and I own The Surefire Group (SFG), a multistate and multimillion-dollar operation that spans multiple industries. SFG currently operates multiple real estate offices, Home Front Mortgage, Keystone State Abstract LLC (parent to nine other title agencies), and a portfolio of over eighty properties. In 2021, I further expanded by acquiring multiple homecare agencies with more than $10 million nationwide gross revenue. I was recently appointed co-chair of the Rising Leaders Committee of R360 and a founding partner, an ultra-high-net-worth club—and the world's most exclusive club—that was recently featured in *Bloomberg Businessweek*.

I find my life today a far cry from my middle-class upbringing. My cop father and teacher mother raised five boys in a northeast Philly row house. I watched my parents work every chance they got, even when my mom got colon cancer. My grandfather eventually moved in with us, which made tight quarters even tighter: eight people in four bedrooms. Although I never lacked anything I needed growing up, I knew from the beginning that I always wanted more. I knew I could do more of everything with money. I could give back, help my family, impact lives, and have freedom.

My family taught me the importance of hard work. They never received any handouts. They never stopped working, and, most importantly, in a house full of eight mouths to feed, if I wanted something that was not necessary to my survival, I had to get it myself. This is by no means a cliché underdog story or an attempt to make you think I had it hard; business is always complicated, no matter where you start. But most people use their upbringing as an excuse to hold them back instead of propel themselves forward. I chose the latter.

My grandfather, James McCabe, passed away in 2019, which got me thinking of all the pearls he had passed along to me. When I was in seventh grade, I went on the trip of a lifetime. My grandfather had moved to Mammoth Spring, Arkansas, onto a twelve-plus-acre farm—a big change from his previous life as a Philly cop,

Inquirer delivery man, and Marine. Talk about the sticks—I thought we would be gun-slinging and billygoat wrestling for the entire trip. He had other ideas! The place was huge, and my grandfather took advantage of the extra help, which meant I had a working trip. I remember him asking what took me so long to complete a farm task he had given me. I began to answer, and he firmly said, "Stop! I don't care what your excuse is, just get it done," then walked away.

I'll never forget that moment or that principle. Results are the only thing people want to see; your sob story has no place in a world fueled only by results. I was lucky enough to be one of the last people to see my grandfather before he passed. When I saw him, I made sure to tell him I was sure God wouldn't hold it against him for being a Marine and not a soldier!

Your sob story has no place in a world fueled only by results.

I have the honor of being a part of a family of fighters, people who put themselves on the line to protect their communities, families, and country. In 2013, I followed the lead of my other grandfather, Charles McBrearty—a Bronze Star recipient from the Korean War—and enlisted in the United States Army. He was my best friend, and even though he had passed away by the time I joined, I wanted him to know that he had raised a fighter. I attribute much of who I am today to the old-school mentality he ingrained in me.

People say my grandfather McBrearty and I were pretty much twins, considering that not only did we look alike, but I also act like him. I really had no friends other than my grandfather, who was in his late seventies and early eighties, for most of my childhood. I would spend hours with him almost every day until he passed away when I was in my mid-teens. One of the best things he taught me was loyalty and trust. He had been in the military and relied on his Army brothers to protect him with their lives, just as they expected him to do the same. He taught me the values of a soldier at a young age.

Now that I am in business, I realize how much that kind of trust speeds up the process in this field as well. I go all-in on trusting people. Life is a sprint; don't be fooled by the "enjoy the journey" people—RUN! If I partner with someone, I trust them 100 percent. And if they fuck me over, that's what an operating agreement is for. You cannot prevent or plan for everything. I will always do what is in the best interest of growing the business, and all involved parties should be on the same page. Worrying about people taking advantage of you only steals your focus.

In 2015, after coming home from Army Basic Training and graduating from Cabrini College with a bachelor's in psychology that I never used, I started selling real estate. This is back when I wanted to be a police officer. I had completed the application process for the Philadelphia Police Department and already had a start date for the academy. By this point, I had been selling real estate for a year and had made about $75,000. It was the most money I had ever made, as my working history up until this point had consisted of minimum-wage retail jobs. I quickly realized that I enjoyed fully controlling my own time and money. I discovered leveraging money and taking full advantage of human capital.

I decided to cancel my application with the Philly PD and purchased my first RE/MAX franchise in 2016. I knew nothing about owning a business or being a real estate broker. I didn't even qualify to take the broker's exam because I had not been in real estate long enough (Pennsylvania requires three years of real estate sales experience to take the exam). None of this stopped me. I never made excuses about not having the right information or not knowing what to do. Instead, I started studying every entrepreneur I could find online. The truth is, all the information you need to be successful is free and easily found on Google or YouTube. You can literally leverage the Internet to learn anything you want for free. If you don't know something, you have chosen not to act and do your own personal research, which, in this day and age, is free to all who have access to the Internet. No one is preventing you from achieving greatness.

When I first opened my RE/MAX franchise, I was a part-time owner. I sold real estate, recruited, cut commission checks, took out the trash, and usually just broke even. I would race the clock every single day, and eventually, I just burned out. The point of beginning this journey had been to achieve freedom, and instead, I was working tirelessly around the clock for minuscule returns.

As fate would have it, I found Grant Cardone on YouTube and immediately signed up for his 10X Growth Conference in Las Vegas and read his book, *The 10X Rule*. Grant's 10X mindset—which says the path to greatness lies in setting goals that are ten times bigger than what you think is possible to achieve and taking ten times the action you feel is needed to accomplish these huge goals—completely changed my outlook on business and life. His content was the mindset shift I needed. It came when I was facing a massive dilemma in my business, as playing jack-of-all-trades was not paying off the way I thought it would, even though it was necessary at the time.

I decided to apply the 10X rule in all aspects of my life, and I never looked back. I stopped selling real estate entirely and gave all my leads to my agents, focusing on recruiting and scaling my office. I would send four thousand emails and text messages every day, offering 95 percent commission to agents. The responses ranged from no response to "fuck you." None of that mattered because I went from five to seventy-five real estate agents in three months! I missed two mortgage payments in the process, but I couldn't have done it any other way. I wanted my business to win, and I was willing to lose everything in return. I realized if I was going to be the CEO, I had to act like one. It was time to go all-in. I now have four locations and over 220 real estate agents, many of whom are top producers, closing over $10 million in sales volume yearly. I have been wholly focused on asset stacking and taking massive action from that point on.

I realized if I were going to be the CEO, I had to act like one.

When COVID-19 hit and crippled many lives and businesses, I took it as an opportunity to grow and scale. Many people have used the pandemic to excuse their lack of achievement—as I write this, they still are—but I did the complete opposite by adopting one of my newer mentalities: *expand while they contract.* Since March 2020, I have closed on four homecare agencies, two RE/MAX offices, fifteen investment properties, and multiple title joint ventures, doing more business and making more money than ever before. I even got married in May of 2021, taking advantage of COVID cancellations and last-minute deals.

Every day, I choose not to let anything get in my way. Over the past two years, my wife and I have traveled to more places and acquired more assets than ever before. We traveled to the Maldives twice, Dubai, Puerto Rico, Necker Island, the Bahamas, Aerial Island, Ireland, and St. Thomas. Think of all the people you know who have put their lives on pause over the past two years. I'm not talking about people with severe medical conditions; I'm talking about competent and fully able-bodied people who just hit pause because the government told them to, acting entirely out of fear. But life goes on, so make sure you keep up and always have control of the reins, as no one else will take you where you want to go.

My aggressive, nothing-can-stop-me, no-bull-shit mentality has rewarded me in many ways. With every action I take, I aim to achieve financial freedom, asset stacking, and high-net-worth networking. Now, I want to outline the fruits of my labor, how I earned them, and teach you the lessons I learned along the way.

Are you ready to execute, dominate, and scale?

CHAPTER 1

THE MIDDLE-CLASS MINDSET

Many of us are raised to be middle-class permanently. Before you read this chapter, know that I have nothing against the middle class. However, if a white picket fence with a thirty-year mortgage and minimum payments on student loan debt for the rest of your life doesn't sound appealing, you'll have to rid yourself of the middle-class mindset! A penny saved is not a penny earned; a penny saved is just a penny. Do you think a billionaire is worried about saving pennies? No! The reality is that you have to spend money to make money.

"The middle-class mindset teaches you to be penny-wise and dollar-poor."

Middle-class equals scared. We are told not to trust strangers and not to work with family. Who does this leave? Seriously, that's everybody! If you can't work with strangers or family, then what are you going to do? Clocking in from nine to five and making $50,000 a year for the rest of your life is scarier than strangers. It is almost impossible to scale your wealth this way; it's hard enough to avoid living paycheck-to-paycheck.

Then you retire and rely on Social Security, which averages about $1,400 per month. I'd rather risk money now to make money later.

MONEY MYTHS

Debt is not a bad thing. Debt is a tool you should want more of, especially in real estate. You can leverage equity to buy more real estate. Here's an example: If you had $50,000 in cash, you could purchase one house that needs a total rehab and hold it as a rental or flip it. Then you have just one property with minimal value and probably not much income. Or you could use that $50,000 to buy *five* $100,000 rental properties using 90 percent bank debt and then pay them down using other people's money over ten years via rent to achieve wealth. Taking advantage of debt opens up earning potential. You can have anything you want—as long as someone else pays for it. Strategize and leverage debt by using others' assets to acquire the property or business. Your ideas coupled with others' resources equals a win-win for all! Middle-class people brag about paying off their student loans, houses, cars, and being debt-free. Rich people call debt *leverage* and use it as a tool to build wealth.

___

**You can have anything you want—
as long as someone else pays for it.**

___

Money won't make you happy. Being broke won't make you happy either. Everyone knows this; it is a stupid and irrelevant comment. Many people suffer because they cannot access things they want and need due to a lack of financial resources. Money pays for food, shelter, and healthcare. You need money. It's interesting when people say things like "Money won't make you happy" because they have no baseline for believing that. How can someone say this if they've never had true wealth? Besides, who said that money and success were everything in the first place? You should immediately assume that a person saying this has given up on any hope of financial freedom.

___

**Poor people pay too much
attention to price and not
enough attention to value.**

___

Save your money. Poor people *save* money; rich people *invest* money. You pay taxes on money you save. Put it to work instead.

Money doesn't grow on trees. Money is printed and is plentiful. Anytime there is a shortage, we print more. If you lack funds, you are not taking enough action.

Only buy something if you get a good deal. Good deals don't always make people rich; big, large-scale deals make people rich. Poor people pay too much attention to price and not enough attention to value. The best deals I have ever made were those I paid a premium for because they pay you back over time.

Don't put all your eggs in one basket. Wall Street sold this popular concept to the middle class to create mutual and index funds. The wealthy don't diversify; they have significant investments in a small number of things. Warren Buffett once said, "Wide diversification is only required when investors don't fully understand what they are doing." Once you establish a fountain of wealth, you can deploy it and diversify by investing in real estate or directly into companies.

FORGET WHAT YOU LEARNED GROWING UP

Pretty much everything you are taught by society is the complete opposite of what you should do to achieve wealth and financial freedom. Over the past six years, I have entirely abandoned every notion about money, wealth, and success that I was taught growing up. Never take financial advice from someone who is broke or caught in the same trap that's laid out for everyone else. Most middle-class people play it safe and have very little faith in themselves or what they can do. They don't ask questions and always wait for perfect conditions instead of taking action *right now*.

In 2016, I charged $1,000 on a credit card for the Grant Cardone 10X Growth Conference in Vegas, and I even flew first class because Cardone says you need to spend a little more to be near quality. I did not meet anyone on the plane, but the lessons I learned at the conference were worth every penny. Middle-class people do not think about the value of flying first class; they think about the price tag. They save a few hundred bucks but lose the opportunity for quality networking, and they are likely not even thinking about the power of human capital.

That $1,000 spent on the conference completely changed my entire life. Ed Mylett and Andy Frisella were speaking, and one of them said something about paying bills and how the middle-class is trained to pay the bills on time and, no matter what, to never ask questions and do whatever the government says. They talked about how this mindset has serious potential to hold you back and prevent you from taking necessary action.

Another speaker at the conference said something that completely changed my way of thinking. I'm paraphrasing, but the gist of it was,

If you're already in a bad spot, if you can't pay the bills, just stop paying and quickly shift gears. Start spending that money on marketing and building, because it will pay back!

Think about it: if you don't have any other option and you're stuck at rock bottom, then what else are you going to do? All I could think as I heard him speak was that it was the worst, most conflicting, and yet best piece of advice I had ever heard. Now, this doesn't mean I'm endorsing not paying your mortgage. This messaging is

aimed at the middle-class, which is tradition-
ally all about paying bills on time, never missing
payments, never accruing debt, and paying off
all debt immediately. However, money spent on
bills won't pay you back. You can keep struggling
to pay your mortgage, or you can change where
you spend your money, temporarily shifting
those dollars to something that has the potential
to earn you more money.

After hearing this advice from the speaker,
I went back to the hotel room and spent all my
money—which was $5,000 at the time—on
Indeed ads, Facebook ads, and a Mailchimp
account that I still use today. I filmed a marketing
campaign, offering agents 95 percent commission and pushed it out until paying for the adver-
tisements depleted my bank account. Nothing
was going to stop me.

Within two months (and two missed mortgage payments later), I had recruited 70 agents.
It increased my income and confidence, and it is
something I never could have done if I had used
my last $5,000 for my mortgage. At this point,
I had already personally stopped selling real
estate, a decision that many real estate brokers
never make—which is why they remain small-
scale real estate brokers who need to produce

for themselves or maintain a sales team that produces. When brokers continue to sell, they do not have time to train their agents, recruit agents, or develop their brokerage. You cannot grow a business if you are focused on other things, and you have to be willing to make sacrifices for the sake of your goals, no matter what they are. I wanted to grow my business, and paying my mortgage would not allow me to do that.

PROXIMITY IS POWER

I remember spending $1,000 on the ticket to the 10X conference, petrified over how I would pay it back. These days, I'm parting ways with $50,000 to see Richard Branson for four days on his private island with R360, an ultra-high-net-worth, invite-only networking group. I don't think a four-day trip is worth $50,000; however, proximity to Richard Branson and R360 members with net worths over $100 million is entirely worth it. I take every opportunity to get closer to people who have done what I want to do. I'm not worth $100 million yet, but I showed them my value, invested my fair share in being a partner, and am now running their Rising Leaders Committee.

Funny enough, my wife and I had a weekend planned in Cape Cod during the dates of the Richard Branson trip. I was pretty annoyed because I lost the $5,000 I had already paid for the trip to Cape Cod, but I knew something amazing would come of the R360 event, even if it took a few years to pay off. I knew the value of being somewhere like that. Ultimately, it paid off *tenfold*.

The group was very intimate, made up of about 25 people, each with a minimum net worth of $100 million. Honestly, I wondered why my wife and I had even been invited. It was intimidating to be around people who had accomplished so much. I grew up middle-class, and my wife grew up lower middle-class. We had no concept of how ultra-high-net-worth people behaved or thought. But I can tell you this: they are ordinary people who put their pants on the same way you do. Everyone was incredibly welcoming and eager to share lessons they'd learned on their journey.

I discovered later that we were invited because Chris Ryan, one of the managing partners of R360, planned to propose that I run a committee within R360 called Rising Leaders. This is a group for the children and heirs of members focused on teaching them how to lead, manage, and invest their inherited wealth properly.

On our first night on Necker Island, we stumbled across an incredibly young face, David Sinclair, PhD. You may be familiar with David as the guy from Harvard who talked about his breakthrough anti-aging research on Joe Rogan's podcast. Ironically, David lives in Cape Cod and invited us to his house. This is how it all comes full circle. It's crazy to think that a Harvard professor who had been on the Joe Rogan show and hangs out with Bill Gates would want to spend time with us, right? Wrong! That's the kind of thinking that will keep you stuck.

Shortly after the trip was over, I received a call from Florence, Chris Ryan's girlfriend, asking if I would be interested in flipping a house with her. I wasn't into flipping houses and didn't trust the market at the time. Nevertheless, I told her I would check it out because it was close by. Once I did, I was in awe. It was listed for $1.4 million and is one of the most beautiful homes I have ever seen. It has stone walls, 9,000+ square feet, and is fully renovated. I told her I wished that it had been five years from now because I wasn't ready to spend that kind of money on a house.

What Florence said next blew my mind. She told me that if I loved the house, I could take it for $1.3 million because the seller was a friend who had to relocate immediately for his position in the military. We bought a house that was appraised for $2.25 million for just $1.3 million in the 2021 real estate market—and this happened less than thirty days after getting home from Necker Island. We now live in a spectacular home, and I now have contacts all over the country from Necker Island. That $50,000 paid for itself in so many ways and has already made us a million dollars in equity.

BE GENUINE

When I meet ultrawealthy people, the only angle I have in getting to know them is that I can hopefully learn something from them that could change my perspective. I'm okay just listening to them and hearing their stories, because their time is valuable. While on Necker Island, attendees kept asking Branson about how space was, which makes no sense because, obviously, space is remarkable. I would have expected these people not to have been intimidated by him and to ask questions of value that would help them establish a relationship with him. I walked up to him and said, "Richard, that was the classiest space launch I have ever seen." That's where we hit it off—he thought I was funny, and his assistant asked for my email. Nothing has come of it yet, but it's pretty cool that his executive assistant has my email. Always do and say things that make you stand out.

While I was there, I established relationships with everyone on the island. The opportunity to go to Necker saved me years of mistakes and will ultimately allow me to propel my businesses and wealth forward at an accelerated rate. Everyone was amazed when they found out I was just twenty-eight years old and from a middle-class background. They thought about what their wealth would look like if they were in my shoes, and they were in awe of how much I was going to grow just because I was there.

Knowing these people will prove extremely helpful to me at some point, even if I don't yet know how, when, or where.

THE BIG RESET

A middle-class mindset is a form of brainwashing akin to chronic disease. Its manifestations affect all aspects of life, and it is nearly impossible to get rid of unless you completely reset your thoughts and actions. This kind of mindset is dangerous because it is disguised as comfortable and stable. Who wants to hear that everything they know about financial success is wrong? That their parents were wrong? That their grandparents were wrong? That everything they are currently doing might be wrong?

The first two business partners I picked were in law enforcement. They both had a salary and were comfortable having something to fall back on; they had a Plan B. One partner eventually took a considerable risk, quit his job, and started doing real estate full-time. We became millionaires together. The other expected returns without putting in the work. One of us was putting in 18-hour workdays, and the other wasn't. I had to force him out of a RE/MAX partnership. The difference between him and me was that I did not make $125,000 a year as a base salary as a police department lieutenant. He was not focused on growing our business, because he felt comfortable with his police job.

That's what the middle-class mindset teaches: to be a *comfortable conformist*. Now, my former business partner is working every day for someone else instead of for himself. But you can't reach above-average levels with jumping all the way in to your opportunities. People are taught to be average, scrape by, and be happy and grateful for what they have. But what do you have if you spend your life having other people always telling you what to do and when to do it?

In today's world, the middle class hides the scarcity mindset, cloaking it in the words *comfort* or *balance*. They even brainwash you to believe that those things are what you should strive for. They think living paycheck-to-paycheck is security because they have been trained to rely on a paycheck. Salaried people are the most at-risk people in a company. They are the first to get cut if there is downsizing or restructuring in the company, especially if they haven't made themselves irreplaceable, which takes more than working just forty hours a week. Salespeople rarely get cut because they work on commission and actually have to work to earn their money.

A while ago, two employees emailed me on a federal holiday to let me know they were in the office and to see if I needed anything. I loved that;

they showed me that they have what it takes to be ultrasuccessful. Off days are chances to get ahead, work while others sleep, and win as others try to catch up. I sent out a message to my real estate agents and salespeople acknowledging the holiday, but more importantly, highlighting the advantages of a federal holiday that no one actually celebrates. It means that Starbucks is empty, and so are the roads. Everyone is at home doing nothing, so call them up. Don't script it, and don't make a spreadsheet about what you will do; none of that matters. Just call them up and talk to them about real estate. Just take action.

The first step to resetting is securing a mentor. If you surround yourself with millionaires and billionaires, you start to believe more in yourself, your businesses, and your strategy because you adopt their *abundance mindset* as your own. To get the most from mentorship, as with most things in life, you have to go all-in. Subconsciously, most people are drawn to others who make them feel comfortable. That is the wrong attitude to use when searching for a mentor! Seeking someone who tells you it's okay to be average will only leave you being average. It's better to look for a mentor who challenges you to grow and constantly seek growth.

Some mentors will tell you to apply and integrate only the things you like from their messaging, but that is not the way it should be. If a billionaire tells you to do something, you should do it. They obviously did many things right, so go all-in in applying their advice until you find another billionaire who closely mirrors your values or goals, then copy what *that* person did. Take advice from people who are not mega-rich if you don't want to be mega-rich. It's simple.

Seeking someone who tells you it's okay to be average will only leave you being average.

Red flags in a mentor include someone who tells you you're doing everything right, who preaches four-hour workweeks, or who gives you any other reason why you shouldn't have to work hard. The truth is, you have to work your ass off. Sure, some people get lucky, but if you're not one of the few, get ready to put everything aside and make space for your priorities. If you are ever perfect or the expert in the room, either someone is lying to you or you are lying to yourself.

The next step is to take action! It's pretty interesting that people go from conference to conference, read hundreds of books, spend tons of money, and never take action. They don't like 100 percent of what they hear, so they don't act on the things that make them uncomfortable. Once you secure your mentor, keep in contact with them. Make them your best friend, and most importantly, get to work.

That is precisely why I buy into what Cardone and Dan Peña (business-mogul-turned-YouTube-savage; warning: don't play his videos around kids) preach. There is no secret recipe, no secret sauce, no shortcuts. Cut the bullshit and get to work. Don't waste time on a spreadsheet, script, or plan. Just get your ideas in motion. I've never been a planner, but I do get shit done. Extensive planning before an idea has even been intro-duced is just a waste of time. The more time you spend withholding your thoughts, the longer it will take for you to take action. Forget what you learned about money growing up, stop looking for perfect timing, surround yourself with people who have ideas, and take massive action.

CHAPTER 2

PRIORITIZE AND EXECUTE

You have to believe in yourself. You have to persist in executing ideas that no one else can see and seem impossible to everyone, including yourself. It is blind faith that will allow you to excel at reaching your goals; you have to believe that things will work out if every action you take is in alignment with your ultimate goals. Prioritizing and executing your list of goals should be the most important thing. If you are in sales, your goal is to sell. You should not be spreadsheeting things; you should be generating income.

If you own a business, your end goal should be cashflow and valuation. Even if you're thinking, "No, the end goal is growth," properly executed growth ultimately equals income. Focus on income-generating activities and delegate everything else. I've noticed many real estate agents making their social media graphics, designing cards, logos, etc., but why? The time spent making graphics could be used to make calls, network, spend time with clients, and actually get things done that directly make money.

The concept of a work-life balance is not an accomplishment. It is a setup for failure and mediocrity.

Remember, you have to spend money to make money. Don't be scared to outsource $10-an-hour work. The person you hire is likely to be better at it than you are anyway. Menial tasks should never be on your priorities list. Free yourself up. I have continually reinvested every dollar I make and have happily stayed broke. I'd rather have more time to focus on my priorities, including scaling and making sure that every company is as big as possible. That is what prioritizing and executing is all about: knowing how to maximize.

THERE IS NO SUCH THING AS WORK-LIFE BALANCE

We must get rid of this myth around work-life balance. Work-life balance is a well-meaning concept that presents itself in many disguises. It's the idea that the stars will align at some point in the future, and you will be able to prioritize your time, energy, and attention between your work and your personal life in perfect proportion. Here is the truth: the concept of a work-life balance is not an accomplishment. It is a setup for failure and mediocrity.

Extraordinary success and achievement require you to be all-in. Amazing things happen with amazing effort. A world-class pianist does not get there by practicing only once a week. This is something you must be conscious of. If you want to make extraordinary things happen, you have to be willing to go all-in and accept that other areas of your life will not always get the attention they deserve.

It is imperative to surround yourself with people who support your goals. You must sell your loved ones on your vision and objectives, and if they genuinely want what's best for you, they will be there no matter how long it takes. When we focus intensely on one area, most other areas of our lives will be at a standstill, hibernating until we're ready to come back to them. Balance does not exist, because when you spend so much time executing in one area, other areas will suffer. If your partner is giving you a hard time about working and is constantly creating conflict, your mind is in the wrong place. This means you did a lousy job selling your vision to your partner, and you need to fix it.

If you spend six years working eighty-hour weeks, your business will grow, but your health may suffer, your sleep will suffer, you'll be less fit than you'd like, and your diet will probably be subpar. Once you're done with that toil, though, you'll be able to focus on everything else and build yourself up. You have to focus on what is most important to you.

I run ten title companies, most of which are joint ventures with other real estate brokers. I am often asked why I choose to work with competitors and why I would want to help them make more money. We don't compete at SFG—we dominate. I am not competing with other brokers, because other brokers don't have ten title agencies. Worrying about competition is thinking small. If you're the big fish, there is no competition. My only concern is about driving more revenue. The more income we have, the more we can accomplish.

Balance does not exist, because when you spend so much time executing in one area, other areas will suffer.

None of this was accomplished with work-life balance. It is incredible what people spend their time on, day in and day out. I work fourteen to eighteen hours a day, and I am not at a point where I think I will ever stop working. My planner is chaotic, filled up every night before I go to bed. I note whatever is on my calendar, including my meetings and so forth. Most days, I take on an extra fifteen to thirty tasks in addition to my scheduled meetings.

How do I get it all done? The most important thing is that I don't procrastinate. That is one of my top priorities. Sometimes, priorities get blurred, and I do get caught up in some administrative matters. But I make sure it gets done the same day if it is written down.

I do all this without beating the sun up. Contrary to what most balance experts suggest, I don't work out at 6:00 a.m. Instead, I work out at night. If something on my calendar or list of tasks does not get done, I do not go to the gym, which is a shame since I love lifting. I think of it as a punishment, a way to hold myself accountable with a built-in reward or punishment.

Everything I do is based on a central philosophy: money first, because money solves everything else. Being the face and revenue generator at SFG and in my personal life takes precedence. It is my strength, and that is what I set out to do every day: prioritize my strengths over everything else.

GET YOUR PRIORITIES RIGHT

There are a lot of people who worry about optics more than they care about actually succeeding and being wealthy. These are the low-performance individuals with a brand-new Mercedes Benz or an equally undeserved flashy item like a Rolex. This drives me insane. Cars, nice suits, and expensive watches are all fluff. I always dress how I want and forgo fancy attire. I wear jeans, shorts, and sometimes sweat-pants to meetings, and I have only one nice watch that I bought on vacation a few years ago. Everything costs money, and I refuse to spend money on useless things or things that someone else is not paying for. A $100,000 car will never make me money, but an extra title processor, agent, investment property, piece of art, or caregiver will.

I refuse to spend money on useless things or things that someone else is not paying for.

Material items and social media allow us to lie to others and ourselves. People present a life full of abundance as vibrant as you can imagine because they are only worried about their image. These same people who put so much effort into their social media probably go to meet clients unprepared with no paperwork and not even a pen. Never be that person. Trust me, your clients will remember your lack of preparedness more than they care or even notice your overposting on social media—daily videos, daily status updates, tons of pictures of themselves but no action, and no money. People making money don't have time for bullshit like social media unless they're making money from it, which the average person is not.

Social media is a huge time waster. The algorithms are literally designed to suck you in and steal your time. Time is money, and I don't particularly appreciate wasting money. I don't even keep social media apps on my phone. Why? Because I know the second someone sends me something to check out, I'll be sucked into the feed and will end up wasting a great deal of time just scrolling away, looking at things that contribute nothing to my goals.

Log on right now and count how many "rich overnight" real estate investors you find. You can probably find ten people who want to "teach" you how to flip houses or invest in multi-family units and storage units. This is one of the scariest things in the real estate market right now. Don't let an Internet wannabee portraying a life filled with jets and luxury cars sell you a $500 course. Only buy into people who have done something. Real estate is and always will be a long-term play. Most people get rich in other business ventures, then deploy their money into real estate for tax advantages, and *then* get wealthy over fifteen to thirty years by holding real estate.

Suppose you've heard that the wealthiest people in the world are in real estate. In that case, you have to remember that the richest people in real estate took thirty to forty years to get there or earned their wealth from a good business *and then* deployed it into real estate by leveraging bank debt and paying it off slowly. Creating wealth is a marathon that should be run as a sprint.

Wealth is built slowly and multiplied using money, not by flipping five houses and making a million dollars in one year. The cash flow on a house flip is terrible because you end up giving half of it to the IRS anyway.

Ask yourself why you want to be in charge of your time and money and enter into the life of a solopreneur. Is it because you have dreams of amassing extraordinary wealth, or is it because you don't want to work hard for someone else? News flash: if you're not a hard worker, you will never be a hard worker unless you have a mindset shift, no matter who you're working for. Don't say you have a business just because you registered an LLC. Businesses have employees, revenue, and expenses. If you want a business, it is your responsibility to make it a successful, cash-flowing business. Everyone wants a get-rich-quick scheme, but most people don't want to do the work.

I'm aggressively patient every day as I'm grinding to scale real businesses while building real relationships with real people. Leave behind the fantasies and get-rich-quick schemes that social media and lame self-help books have sold you. You need to focus on revenue, scale up, and build a team with systems aimed at performance and growth. A business also makes cash, has real people, and provides real value. The point of growing a company should be to build something so significant that it allows you to exit later with a fortune. So, whatever it is you're doing, make it bigger.

There are 31.7 million small businesses in America, out of which around 20 percent are solopreneurs who do not have even one employee.[2] People are being encouraged to be solopreneurs and start their own business with the wrong goals in mind. Why work for someone else when you can make yourself rich? Becoming a solopreneur does not make you wealthy. You are more at risk for becoming broke when you leave the security of a nine-to-five behind. Not everyone has what it takes to run a business. That's why they fizzle out most of the time.

I think a lot of people are drowning in mediocre successes. Every day is a new day, a new chance to make millions. If I set up a title business today for $100 million, yes, it would be awesome, but tomorrow I will strive for another. I don't stop or slow down. I continue and use the momentum to press on. Success is like a glass of champagne—sip it and move on. Sometimes I feel like I condense what most people do in a week into one day. Maintaining your gear is all about overcommitting and executing on everything you have promised to yourself and others. Make sure you have something going on every hour and that anything you put in your planner, no matter how small, is executed or delegated to someone who can get it done.

A lot of this mindset is thanks to my time in the military and not wanting to be a burden to my team. Prioritizing and executing, in general, is as simple as getting day-to-day stuff done. It starts with waking up early, having your clothes ready, charging your electronics, not going to an appointment without a contract or a pen, and so on. You would not believe the number of times I have seen people asking clients for a pen. Success isn't only about planning and executing on the business end; it is about always being prepared so you can make the most of your time and your day. The little things are a sign or even a symptom of who you are on the inside. How you do one thing is how you'll do everything.

How you do one thing is how you'll do everything.

When I was selling real estate, I used to win listings because, as per my clients, I had a presentation, multiple pens, and contracts ready for execution. I came to close. Most of the time, I was up against neighborhood career agents who had been in the business for twenty years but were just full of themselves and got complacent. They knew their name was all over the neighborhood, so they felt that all they had to do was show up, and that's all it would take for them to get a listing.

Everything you do should contribute to your bottom line, and unfortunately, people can't even get small shit together. If your phone is chronically not charged, if you're constantly losing your keys or credit cards, if you can't wake up early, start there before moving on. Large-scale growth requires your full attention, and little distractions will get in your way. This is the wrong kind of chaos and a telltale sign of a lack of discipline that will leave you with average accomplishments.

Next time you feel like you don't want to do something, do it anyway. Tell yourself that you'll rest tomorrow; that's the only thing I advocate putting off until the next day. Get up today and get it done. You have to hold yourself accountable, so stop relying on perfect conditions that are never coming or on other people for help. Doing so gives external circumstances and other people so much power over you. I don't know about you, but I like to be in control. You are the only person in control of your life, and you have to accept that for the double-edged sword that it is. You are just as responsible for a prosperous life as you are for a life that goes to hell. So, before you set out to get shit done, square yourself away, be presentable, and be prepared.

A team's success depends on the leader's willingness to take the blame for failure. Therefore, as a leader, be prepared to accept responsibility. If everyone is following your example, you need to set the bar for taking the blame. But at the same time, be ready to identify where you made mistakes so you don't make them again, and make sure your team knows why you're pivoting. Agreement is always an option, but commitment is not.

You are just as responsible for a prosperous life as you are for a life that goes to hell.

Influential leaders mitigate risks before a mission or project begins, but they don't procrastinate. Evaluate the problem, develop a solution, and direct the execution. Then move on! When the priorities shift, don't forget to communicate, and don't get caught up in the trap of tunnel vision by focusing on one priority. This will only lead to target fixation, preventing you from seeing the bigger picture.

Leaders must make a call and take action over and over again. Your plan is useless, your degree is worthless, and your words are useless without action. Remember that actions eventually become instinctual when you empower yourself.

BUILD RELATIONSHIPS THE RIGHT WAY

The team always gets to eat first, and I'll eat last. If you take care of your crew, your crew will take care of you and your business. When I bought the last three RE/MAX franchises, I purposely put myself in a position that was not personally advantageous. I didn't take any financial disbursements for myself for three quarters. Instead, I gave it back to my shareholders and paid them back much earlier than agreed on. I wanted them to believe in me and know that believing in me pays.

The minute I came back from Necker, I was flooded with calls from people trying to get me to pitch deals to the people I had met on the island. This is the wrong approach. I wasn't interested in using their money; I was more interested in getting close to them and learning about how they earned their money, their thought processes, what they did for fun, how they treated their family, etc. There is plenty of money out there; what is scarce is access to people with money.

Think about it: I had just met these people, so the priority was building a relationship with each one of them. Practicing anything else is a scarcity mentality—you know, the mentality that makes you think the pot of money is getting smaller and smaller each time someone takes from it. The goal should be to invest your time in people you can learn from so they then feel comfortable investing in you. Besides this, at twenty-eight years old, I was the youngest person on Necker Island. How would it look if I started calling these people to invest in a deal they had zero interest in and that was way below the scale they were working on? Build the relationships and find bigger deals.

The ideal scenario is to develop so much trust that they feel comfortable coming to me for ideas about deals. To create that kind of relationship, you first show your value. Of course, there are times when people move as fast as me and want to do business right away, and I always take advantage of the momentum and do it. It's brilliant if it happens. But I am just as content to be on the phone with them only to learn what they were working on and learn how I could help them get to the next level. The goal, once again, is to build relationships and see where I can be valuable. Building relationships is as simple as sending out occasional texts to keep in touch. Slow relationship-building always wins.

Ultimately, relationships are where the most value comes from.

Most people look to make a quick buck, like a one-night stand for deals. They think all it takes is a good idea and a pitch. Most high-network people don't have a shortage of deals; they care about fostering relationships. Executing is not about soliciting someone you just met yesterday to try and get a deal done; it is all about doing things to add value to their lives to ensure they stay in your life. A lack of effort could rub the high-value people the wrong way.

While I stress prioritizing revenue each day, strong relationships are a funnel to more revenue. Ultimately, relationships are where the most value comes from. Knowing the right people can produce something huge, whether in six months or even a year.

Most things you do will not work out, which is why it is crucial to plan and execute as much as you possibly can because, technically, the laws of the universe are against you. Richard Branson started around three hundred businesses, and only seventy became successful. This is fine, because failures don't matter when you're taking massive action. Move so quickly that you don't even realize your losses. I don't address my failures because I don't need any extra negativity in my life. It's all about mindset.

I've always relied on the principle of "hire fast, fire fast," because your chances of success with that person or the next hire are the same. It doesn't matter if you do it slower or faster. The slow method will only allow you to find more barriers because you could be stuck with a poor-performing employee. This isn't rocket science but simple, service-based business knowledge. For some reason, everyone wants to be a rocket scientist at whatever they are doing.

When I hired Jadah Hill to run our title sales operation for me, she was bcc'd on an email about an agent being fired. She immediately responded that she had never met a broker who fired an agent. My response was that other brokers must be scared and desperate because they don't have enough income. I fired our top agent, someone who had even been on the cover of a magazine featuring top producers. Get with it or get lost. If you are going to call and complain about every single thing that happens in this company, then you don't belong here. I want to have self-sufficient people. I would rather have one person who works hard than five who are a pain in the ass.

You don't need to be a rocket scientist; you need to get it done. Whether it is recruiting enough people, raising money, getting your product to people, or making enough phone calls, speed is of the essence. Again, the *best-known* product will always beat the *best* product. Coca-Cola might not even be as good as some other cola brand that we don't even know of because Coca-Cola dominates the market.

In September of 2021, my executives and I were at a Cardone mastery event in Miami. There was a young kid around thirteen years old in the crowd, and Cardone brought him up on stage. He asked the kid if he had a business, to which the boy replied that he didn't. Grant then asked what he would do if he had one, and he said he could fix cell phones. Cardone asked him *how* he would fix them and if he had a method or technique. The kid said he didn't know how he could. Immediately, Cardone announced to the crowd that he wanted to fund this kid's business with $100 per head. With no product or business plan, the child raised $3,500. When Cardone was handing him the money, he presented the kid with two options: either take the money now and walk away or give it back to him and he would double it by December. The boy decided to let Grant double it. Smart kid. This taught this young entre-preneur the importance of *reinvesting*. It was amazing to see this happen, and it is a real-life example of how you don't even need a product or a plan. All you need to do is get out there. All that matters is taking action.

Executing on a day-to-day basis is all about lining up your priorities and creating momentum. If you are doing everything you know you are supposed to do, you feel good and feel that you have achieved something. This involves rebranding and retraining yourself to create a new identity as a person who always accomplishes what they set out to do.

CHAPTER 3

THERE IS NO SHORTAGE OF MONEY

People readily believe they are going to make $50,000 a year when they get out of college, as we in Western society are led to believe that we are nothing without a college degree. The reality is that most college graduates are putting themselves in a box that limits their earnings for life. On top of crushing college debt, they limit themselves to thinking they can only perform in the area where they have been pigeonholed and likely salaried. This is middle-class thinking, and honestly, it's just plain sad. I'm not knocking college, but I am criticizing the thought process that leads people to think they are worth a set figure for the rest of their lives.

Almost immediately after I began selling real estate as a new agent, I started writing offers on one-hundred-property portfolios, making at least three hundred and fifty offers per year. I had this idea that if the seller gave me seller financing of 100 percent, with me paying $0 at closing, I could refinance in six months and buy it at a 20 percent discount. If this worked, there was no way I could lose. I was even willing to go as far as letting the seller keep all the rental income, keep their management in place, and so much more.

Even though I had nothing to lose, it still wasn't easy. There were days when I was laughed at on calls for even pitching this idea. It was *that* crazy and unheard of. But believe it or not, after making close to three hundred and fifty offers, I came across interested sellers. They were three attorneys who owned properties together in Pittsburgh but were not seeing eye to eye with each other on other fronts, and they wanted to get rid of their portfolio in a hassle-free way.

I had just scored a deal with literally no money. We've all heard of the concept of OPM—other people's money; well, it was about to work for me on a vast scale. Now, I just needed $20,000 to cover the cost of appraisals. I was fortunate that Karl Schnitzer, who grew up around the corner from me, reached out over Facebook to tell me he was looking to buy a duplex. Call it fate, but none of this would have happened if Karl hadn't reached out. He had exactly the amount of money needed for the appraisals. I told him about the deal, and he was in. It was a no-brainer—$20,000 down for one duplex, or go in with me on seventy-five properties. Some people would have been scared of a deal so large and so different, but Karl knew he was going to spend his $20,000 regardless, so he took a leap of faith. What started as a bonkers concept ended up getting us seventy-five properties that were 100 percent seller-financed! I refinanced them a year and a half later, and I walked away with a $70,000 commission out of that deal. Out of one deal!

The point here is that creativity and persistence pay off. There is no cap on the money you can make or raise. If you aren't thinking big enough or creatively enough, you aren't going to convince people to go for something like this. People tend to get nervous about seller financing because it does not make any sense to them. The simplest way to explain it is that the seller is the bank. No matter how big the deal is, I know seller financing is possible because I've done it time and time again. I built a $15 million homecare company in nine months in 2021 using seller financing. These deals may not always be the best, but a huge deal can get done with virtually no money out of pocket. I got seventy-five properties this way. Most people can't even get that with a bank loan!

There is a misconception that there's a cap on the money to be made, but that's false. It's a lie that people believe because they lack the creativity or the ability to solve problems. Not having any money right now doesn't mean you can't acquire money or learn how to acquire massive amounts of money. You need to get creative when putting deals together in a way that allows everyone to win. And more importantly, you need to get ready to ask for deals or funding, or whatever it is you're looking for, over and over again until you get a *yes*.

Most people never start their own business or jump into commission-only sales because they don't want to lose their slow-growing nine-to-five job security. They want to hold on to perceived safety, so they either stay in their salaried job and never venture into independent income generation, or they become half-hearted independent income generators (i.e., part-time agents). A half-hearted effort never produces fruitful results. These part-timers never make it; they either regress to safety or they take a leap of faith by believing in themselves and making the switch to full-time.

A half-hearted effort never produces fruitful results.

I am not the broker who lies to agents by telling them they can earn serious money by selling real estate on the side. Part-time agents don't make six figures; in my experience, they rarely close on anything. There are certain instances when you may make money if you're selling to people you know. But after this momentum dies down, it's up to you to create more. How can that happen if you have only one foot in the door?

So, why don't people take the jump? It is all about the fear of being unemployed and the assurance of a paycheck that hourly and salaried jobs provide that give people a false sense of job security. They want to be safe and stay in their comfort zone. Sure, certain law enforcement and healthcare jobs don't carry an ever-looming threat of being fired. But ultimately, the only true security is that which you create for yourself by always maintaining complete control.

GET BIGGER PROBLEMS

Once you decide to fully commit yourself to growth, the numbers game will make or break things for you. If you want to grow, you have to do more. Shake more hands, meet more people, set up more phone calls, propose more deals, and continue to do more and more of everything. The level of chaos in your schedule will ultimately dictate how much money you make. No matter the line of business, the key to success is to make yourself known. As a new broker, I fervently called as many agents as I could. I wanted as many people as possible to remember me and know I was in business—even if they didn't contribute to my goals at that moment. More phone calls inevitably equal more deals. If you haven't seen the kind of growth or income you're looking for, it means you're not spending your time wisely or productively.

People dislike my aggressive approach to business and recruiting; I take it as a signal that I'm doing the right things. Ordinary people are worried about offending people and what others think of them. They are fearful of being disliked or outright hated. I must have been at some point too; everyone has this fear. But I would rather contact a hundred agents and have some of them hate me while still bringing a portion of them into my brokerage every month. I'm not going to lose any sleep if I get ignored or if they don't know anything about me aside from the fact that I am persistent and don't take no for an answer. The truth is, I will always be there in their inbox because always being in touch results in new relationships, and new relationships equal money.

Don't get too obsessed with relationships, and don't put all your eggs in one basket by focusing too much on the same people. Volume is a crucial ingredient for growth; no matter how good your relationships are with a few people, significant gains come from being in touch with a *multitude* of people. Sure, your clients can love you, but love won't keep you from being broke. I want my clients to love me and refer business to me because I did my job and executed my promises. I don't think business associates need to know about your family, interests, and so on right away. You are only hurting yourself in the short term if you believe otherwise, because nurturing relationships that won't go anywhere is a waste of time.

I was recruiting agents and loan officers, setting up title ventures, and working on home-care deals when I decided that, in order to push SFG to the next level, I needed more people to do exactly what I was doing while also leveraging their relationships on the company's behalf. I decided to hire a manager for RE/MAX who used to be at Keller Williams Realty. His responsibilities include being the main point of contact for agents and recruiting. I then shifted my focus to growth and focused only on asset staking and recruiting. A few months after my manager settled in, I hired someone to focus solely on business development. Their job is literally to go to events, mingle, meet new people, get our name out there, and make contacts. There are roughly four thousand real estate agents in the MLS, and most of them are contacted by one of my recruiters or me.

CREATE VALUE

I recently had a sales meeting with employees of my title companies, and I asked how many of them felt like they were stuck because they are salaried employees. A couple of brave people raised their hands. But the thing is, they're *not* stuck. I know, because I own the company and set it up to encourage every employee to add extra value and thereby create extra income for themselves. If they bring in the title business, I pay up to 25 percent commission on top of their salary. This is something they all know from the moment they are hired. The opportunity to earn is available to everyone. Are you actually stuck, or are you not taking advantage of an opportunity?

I even view competition as an opportunity. There is no shortage of real estate brokers. I don't get hung up on the competition; I *service* the competition. I have joint ventures with brokers throughout the country. That is creating value. Where other people see defeat, you need to see opportunity.

There are innumerable ways to make money in real estate. As an agent, I sought to offset the cost of everything, even fuel. Selling a home warranty put $50 in my pocket, and that is about what it took to fill my gas tank. Refer, refer, refer—and never do it for free. You may not be getting cash from each referral, but referrals should be treated like transactions in which something is exchanged. Maybe a referral to one person earns you a connection by them to that developer you've been wanting to meet. Market your knowledge and connections to gain more knowledge and connections. Referring is a great way to create value because the act of referring is covered in the guise of helpfulness. People will be happy with you for helping them out and be more willing to give you something in return.

CHAPTER 4

SET MASSIVE GOALS

If you are not generating enough income, you're not thinking big enough! Not meeting goals sees its roots in either not taking enough action, leading to a small pipeline, or inefficient systems, leading to missed opportunities. I got my start in real estate and have capitalized big-time on something that most brokers already do. Many brokers already have a title company and a mortgage company in addition to their brokerage. What I am doing is not rocket science. Typically in this setup, the real estate brokerage feeds in-house deals to the title and mortgage companies, which generate no other income other than that which relies on the brokerage's agents. I didn't like this model, as this was a very limited setup, and saw no reason why these two completely separate entities could not produce independently. My ancillary companies are standalone companies that service many "competing" brokers through joint ventures and operate in standalone locations in many states. SFG real estate, title, and mortgage services are diversified, scaled, and each company can run itself. The failure of one would never affect another. Never allow one company to solely determine the success of another.

Let's face it: most people are okay with being average. Why? Because they become saturated by mundane, run-of-the-mill standards by surrounding themselves with people who have unremarkable accomplishments. We all know people who make just enough money to get by and are stressed about money yet do nothing to change their situation, as if complaining will do it for them. There is nothing wrong with being broke; everything is wrong with staying broke.

To think bigger, you need to surround yourself with people who are unimpressed with your work ethic. Create an environment for yourself that forces you to grow. If your friends all make about the same as you, less than you, or spend their time doing wasteful things like playing video games, watching TV, or whatever else people do to waste their twenty-four hours, get new friends! You can't have a mindset shift if you constantly surround yourself with uninspiring people. People tend to overestimate their abilities, influence, and work ethic, which is easy to do if your social circle is made up of complacent time-wasters and nearly impossible if you're surrounded by people with extraordinary accomplishments. Stop lying to yourself.

I set unreasonable and irrational goals year after year, and I realize they are still not big enough because I keep crushing them. My healthcare partners and I set a goal of $8 million in revenue over five years, and we did that in six months! Growing up, you're told not to set the bar too high, that you should always under-promise and overdeliver, and so on. Taking a page from Cardone, I always overpromise and overdeliver—every time. No matter what your industry is, if you are getting shit done repeatedly, you will succeed.

I write my goals down every year, looking back at the ones I wrote down the year before. My first goal was to have a net operating income of $500,000, which I'm proud to say that I have crushed by more than double. Next, I wanted one hundred and sixty-five agents doing a hundred transactions a month. My brokerage is now doing three hundred transactions with two hundred agents (remember, I started off in 2016 with only five agents). Then, I set out to get a marketing and transaction coordinator. Done! I wanted a real estate brokerage volume of $125 million, and guess what? The brokerage does $450 million in volume.

If I had fallen short of this $125-million-vol-ume-per-year goal, I would have disappointed myself even though these goals are enormous compared to what most people come up with. This disappointment would have been a driving force for an even bigger plan. Most people don't even have articulated goals. Think about what you want, actually write it down, then rid yourself of limiting beliefs and make those goals even bigger. When your goal is huge, you must take colossal action to accomplish it. You likely won't fail, and even if you fall short of a massive stretch goal, you'll still be satisfied and will have learned a lot to help you crush it the next year. I should have been writing bigger goals five years ago; I should have said I wanted to do $2 billion in real estate volume.

Now, my goals include owning every title joint venture in the country. Many title companies are outdated, out of touch, and definitely not servicing their people properly. It is easy money for me to pick up the slack and acquire their customer base. All I have to do is wait for existing contracts with their clients to end or wait for a broker who is frustrated enough to break their contract and risk a lawsuit to make double the income. This does happen, and I always advocate for it. Make millions but have to pay a couple of thousand in legal fees? It should be a no-brainer.

Another goal I've written down is to own four hundred units, each cash-flowing at least $300 a month. I have not executed this goal post-pandemic, though, because the market does not support it. You cannot control some things, and it is wise to recognize that. I won't allow someone to tell me I am overreaching or dreaming too big, but I will never overpay.

Setting your goals is vital because it allows you to leverage your time properly and bring on support people when necessary. Another one of my goals in 2020 was to acquire $8 million in revenue at a 10 percent margin on the homecare side. We are operating closer to 30—40 percent margins, depending on the company, and doing $15 million in revenue. I did not do any of that on my own! I identified the goal and quickly identified all the people who could help me reach that goal, including a comanaging partner and a CEO, Michael Ferraina. My daily involvement ends with deal structuring. I focus on acquisition and expansion. I talk about homecare every Friday at 8:30 a.m. for thirty minutes, yet I still managed to exceed my goal by doing $15 million in revenue in six months.

I hired Mark Moses, founder of CEO Coaching International, who I met on Necker Island, to coach my team. Mark is an incredibly focused individual, and having the opportunity to know him had a massive impact on my executive team. I was telling him about my newly hired chief of staff, and he looked at his résumé and immediately said that he wasn't a chief of staff but a chief operating officer. It took him seconds to make that suggestion. He pointed out that he was an operator in the military and Army special forces, so I would get more out of him as a COO. Coming from a guy who has been there and done that, I didn't even think twice about changing his role and responsibilities to fit a position that would better suit him and the organization.

You are only one person, and even if you are working every single second, you will not grow to extraordinary levels unless you outsource. I now have some form of executive running each of my businesses. These are individuals I have coached to make the decisions for me. I communicate with them daily, and hiring them has freed up my time to focus on scaling each business.

EASY ISN'T WORTH IT

Never set a goal that doesn't excite you. An easy goal won't get you out of bed in the morning. Making $50,000 a year at a job you hate is doable . . . and pretty loathsome. Gyms are packed for the first two weeks of every year. Then, the "resolutioners" get back to their couches, and the dedicated get their gym back. The resolutioners made a last-minute, poorly defined goal to get in shape. There is likely no emotional attachment to the goal, nor was it big enough or well-defined enough to keep their attention. You have to write your goals down every day so you have constant reinforcement and repeat them as if they have already been achieved (i.e., *I am* _____ or *I have* _____). Speak your goals into existence.

Start by writing down a vision of your ideal life and everything you have to do to achieve every aspect of your vision or goal. Then identify all the things you have to do daily to achieve your goal. Finally, and this is the most important part, get to work every day on accomplishing the tasks that will take you closer to achieving your goals. Knowing what to do by itself is worthless; taking action is what creates results. You can establish a rhythm, and it's funny how this constant movement will eventually make you feel like shit when you don't get things done.

Most people don't set big goals because they are afraid of criticism. Ultimately this fear of criticism of the unknown makes you apprehensive about setting any goal, even small ones. Next thing you know, you're struggling with anxiety and losing your mind over a to-do list that consists of dropping something off at the post office, going to the grocery store, and making dinner. I firmly believe that very few people have actual, intractable clinical depression or anxiety. But the pharmaceutical companies and doctors receiving kickbacks keep marketing it. We push people to call a doctor or take medication because they're "feeling overwhelmed" instead of teaching them coping mechanisms, let alone teaching them how to get ahead.

No one is addressing the cause of depression or anxiety. Treatment includes, "Take this pill... oh, it didn't work? No problem, try this other pill." Did anyone ever think to try circumventing the purposelessness that fuels anxiety and depression by enforcing taking action and control? After all, isn't anxiety feeling out of control? Maybe it is, because they are not doing anything with themselves to grab control. If I weren't doing anything, then I would be anxious too, and I would say one of my greatest drivers is the anxiety that I'm not doing enough. The wallowing in self-pity needs to stop and especially needs to stop being encouraged by society. If I was taught to watch out for sticks and stones *and* words, I would feel crippled. Why are we teaching our kids to be offended by everything? It doesn't make any sense; we should be teaching resilience.

Set the goal and get to work because, at the very least, it will distract you from other bullshit in your life. Once you figure out what you want, make it bigger. Write down all your ridiculous goals as if they have already come to fruition. It gets you motivated and fires you up and ready to pursue it. It forces you to get creative and think outside the box. It also fires up other people around you (of course, only if they're the *right* people).

People who set a $10 million goal and hit only one-tenth of that goal are so much further along than people who set and meet $500,000 goals.

I wrote a goal back in January 2021 that I wanted to meet a billionaire. In March or April of

2021, I went to an event in Georgia where I hit it off with a senior partner of a tax strategy firm. It turns out he has a billionaire client who has a presidential art collection similar to mine. I expressed my interest in meeting him and was soon disappointed that his client thought it would be a waste of time to meet with me. That was okay because I was undeterred in my goal to meet a billionaire. Fast-forward about thirty days later, when I got invited to Necker Island. I met multiple billionaires, including Richard Branson, an incredible entrepreneur whose business philosophy I admire.

People who set a $10 million goal and hit only one-tenth of that goal are so much further along than people who set and meet $500,000 goals. It all boils down to shifting your perspective on winning and losing. Technically, I didn't lose that opportunity to meet with the first billionaire. Instead, I took advantage of more opportunities to meet wealthy people.

100 PERCENT SELLER FINANCING

When I started writing this book, I wanted to give good examples of what can be done when your goals are big enough. In 2016, when I first got into real estate, I met a guy who ultimately changed my life. Robert Mazer of Mazer Real Estate is a broker and developer from Philadelphia. He is in his nineties now and a prime example of a mentor who is worth going all-in on. Bob has had many successful businesses in the lending and real estate space, and all his kids have achieved amazing things.

I was lifting weights at Northeast Racquet Club when Bob walked up to me and joked about working-in, or going next, in gym slang. Now, an eighty-three-year-old man was not really going to work-in on a 315-lb. bench press. But I liked his sense of humor and no bullshit attitude, and we hit it off. I told him I had just gotten licensed to sell real estate, and he said he had been in real estate for years. Call it fate. I immediately said I wanted to learn how to build a thousand-unit portfolio and flip homes. He told me something incredible: "Joe, only three things sell a home: price, location, and condition. Only one of those things can change easily—the price. Go sell twenty-five homes, learn the value of real estate and how to work with people, and I have a surprise for you." I sold twenty-five homes within a few months while an agent at Keller Williams Langhorne, and then I called Bob.

We met at Cin Cin, a Chinese restaurant in Chestnut Hill, Philadelphia, and his favorite place. Bob was the first wealthy person I had ever really met, and man, he was different. He was kind, he tipped well, and everyone knew him. He was like a celebrity in that restaurant. We sat down, and he handed me a spreadsheet with one hundred renter-occupied homes on it and said, "Do you think you could sell this?" In typical Joe fashion, I said, "Hell, yes." I ran with it. We got so close with many buyers, but they would always have a $10,000–100,000 deficit that no one would budge on. Then, I got an idea: I told Bob he could give 100 percent seller financing on these properties to *me*, keep the deed in escrow, manage, hold all profit in an escrow account, and after the six-month seasoning was up, I would refinance. He thought it was an incredible idea, and we got to work.

This was a long-term investment, and I didn't want the cash flow. I just wanted to pay down debt over thirty years without too much of an up-front investment. I had this deal fully approved with Finance of America Commercial when his partner blew up the contract and decided to renovate the units and sell them retail, a project they are still working on today.

I'm sure his partner was scared I couldn't pull it off. I love Bob, and we still own a plane together even though this deal fell through. It allowed me to build a relationship with him and eventually laid the foundation for the deal I seller-financed in Pittsburgh.

I had a chip on my shoulder and something to prove. I was pissed about losing this deal, but I had zero dollars. I started writing offers on portfolios of more than one hundred properties, asking for the same terms all over the country. Talk about hate; people thought I was insane and a fool for writing these offers. As I mentioned in a previous chapter, I was writing hundreds of offers at this time. I knew if I got enough *no* replies, someone would eventually say *yes*. To give you more detail on the deal, it was a combination of three merged portfolios combining more than a hundred units. We got all three portfolios under contract, and, in the end, Karl and I owned eighty properties with zero deposit valued at more than $4.5 million. And because I always capitalize on everything, I was due a 3 percent commission on the $3 million deal after the refinance.

I knew this was a once-in-a-lifetime opportunity, and I had to get it done. I called Karl, asked him routine questions that I would ask a client to preapprove them, and then said, "How about buying one hundred properties instead of one?" I explained this situation. Thankfully, he liked me and was hungry for more, so he said yes! We then spent the next year completing the deal and stabilizing the units. We started with a hundred, but some did not meet the lender's minimum loan amount of $50,000, so we had to drop them. I have applied this exact model on over eighty properties, two home health-care companies, one RE/MAX office, and one title agency. Again, there is no shortage of money. You're just not thinking big enough.

PROVE YOUR WORTH

My executive team had a meeting scheduled with a couple of real estate agents who weren't using our title companies but had been grandfathered in on our commission plans. Our relationship is a business relationship, and we were overdelivering. My approach with them was that if I have to give, they too have to give. Jadah Hill, who runs business development for title, called to tell me that one of the real estate agents she had met with was mad at me. Why? Because I did not ask her personal questions; I hadn't gotten to know her. I had an answer for her she didn't want to hear. I called the agent and told her I wanted to give her some feedback. I told her that if she wanted me to ask about her family the next time, she needed to get on my radar and sell more. I had this conversation with her, knowing it would probably make her leave the brokerage. That was fine; we are one big team, and everyone needs to be on the same page. If someone on the team is a virus, we cut them out fast. She wasn't selling enough, so she shouldn't expect to be rewarded in a sales position. If you want someone to know you, be worth knowing.

This isn't meant to be mean, but it is a statement of fact: be worth knowing, provide value, recognize that no one owes you anything, and earn everything. While on Necker Island, one woman casually joked that she subsidized my wife's and my ticket for the event—an assumption inspired by my age. It was a pretty shitty thing to hear and something I have constantly struggled with. Being the youngest person in the room among big players is something most people can't fathom. I quickly corrected her, explaining that I had paid full price just like her and everyone else. Today, we now have a relationship born from mutual admiration. She is a fantastic businesswoman who had a recent multi-hundred-million-dollar exit.

There is this unfair assumption that if you're young, you're a broke person who has no value. I vividly remember the first time someone called out my age. In 2016, I was interviewing a real estate agent, and at the end of the interview, he said, "Aren't you too young to own all of this? You have no experience." My response was, "Well, if I'm too young and you have all the experience, aren't you too old not to own it yourself? Not to mention you came to me for the interview." We never spoke again. He wasn't a cultural fit or a big thinker. I don't care if I make people uncomfortable because I have earned my place at the table. I built it myself.

FIND YOUR INSPIRATION

Honestly, I don't love title insurance, home health care, or real estate. I love the life it provides for me and everyone who works with me. I love that every day is different and I love solving problems; the industries we are in could be anything and I would feel the same. My goal is freedom, so I am constantly hunting for things that create independence. Freedom to me is the ability to do anything I want, have anything I need, travel anywhere I want to go, be connected to the most affluent people in the world, and help anyone I want to help with my resources. That's why I've decided not to play small and scale everything up. To have freedom, I need multiple self-sustaining companies that could run without me and independently of each other.

Freedom to me is the ability to do anything I want, have anything I need, travel anywhere I want to go, be connected to the most affluent people in the world, and help anyone I want to help with my resources.

I have recently focused on growing my title business because so many other title companies are playing small. The hardest part is getting in front of a broker, which is becoming easier as I expand my business development office. Our joint venture setup is simple: don't settle for a kickback, become an owner, do all the work, and the broker gets paid more than whatever they were getting before. This is why we are crushing our competitors. I am good at structuring deals, and I make it so that my partners don't have to worry about anything on the back end. The key to staying motivated is to find what you're good at. Always remember you don't have to love what you do, but you do have to work so hard that you love what it can provide.

CHAPTER 5

PICK A MENTOR AND GO ALL-IN

Never take advice from someone you wouldn't trade places with. A person who is struggling to pay their bills shouldn't be giving financial advice. The beauty of mentorship is that it speeds everything up—as long as your mentor is worth listening to and learning from. Knowing a super-successful person who has worked their ass off allows you to circumvent a multitude of shitstorms.

Mentorship can take a variety of forms: watching videos and presentations online, reading books, and building relationships in person. Ideally, you want to find someone you can access in real life because this will allow you to pick their brain and receive criticism and live advice. The problem with supplemental forms of mentorship is that they are self-interpreted. There is no one responding to you from a video to correct you if you think achieving freedom means you should prioritize your free time. In order to get the most from videos and books, you already have to be on the right track and use those resources as ammo. My suggestion is to find someone you can create a relationship with and learn from in real time.

Once you identify a worthy mentor, you have to consciously decide to follow their advice. It doesn't matter that you know Warren Buffett if you do nothing to capitalize on the relationship. Your mentor should have success in an area you desire to grow in. Read that again: your mentor should have success in an area you desire to grow in. This means that you don't need to agree with all their opinions. If you pick a mentor with opposing political opinions, just don't talk about politics. Honestly, even if *they* talk about politics, you shouldn't air *your* opinion. You are creating this relationship to better yourself in a specific area, not to get political advice. Just don't have that conversation, plain and simple. Or be open to others' opinions and strong enough to politely challenge them. Recognize your role in the relationship, and don't get in your own way.

Your mentor should have success in an area you desire to grow in.

YouTube is free, and audiobooks are cheap. Use these abundant resources to get yourself in the right frame of mind and go all-in. If Cardone, Dan Peña, Ed Mylett, and Andy Frisella all say to write down five things, write down ten. That's the level of dedication following your mentor and your goals needs to be given. Remember, you can always pay to be around these people, and it's worth paying to be around these people.

Believe it or not, I have never lost money by paying for an event. Never! I've actually made $1 million in equity in my own house by spending $50,000 to go to Necker Island. This was not an amount I was prepared to spend, and I had to spend a number of weeks convincing myself and my wife that it would be worth it. She thought I was crazy!

Anyone who has done something you want to do is valuable. Don't get caught up in the areas where you disagree because you don't want to replicate that stuff anyway. I think Tony Robbins has a lot of great things to say, but the spiritual, mushy side is a slight turnoff for me so I just don't listen to that part. But if Tony Robbins tells me something to do with money, then boom, I'm sold!

Focus on the areas you wish to replicate and expand on. People lose interest in valuable mentors because of stupid shit all the time. A while back, people were outraged when Grant Cardone announced he was going bankrupt. How could this guy who has made a name for himself giving business advice be going bankrupt? People were pissed and vowing to strip themselves of all his teachings.

What was actually going on was a ploy for publicity. Someone was heckling him in the comments, calling him fake and saying he would probably go bankrupt, so he rolled with it. He posted a video on YouTube announcing his bankruptcy and offering all of his stuff for pennies on the dollar. Soon after, he announced that it was fake and merely a response to a heckler who was berating him nonstop. He said his operations team thought he had lost his mind. At the end of this, he gained a million followers in a week. Very smart.

He was being criticized by people who have maybe one hundred followers and have no idea what they were talking about, while he was generating success and wealth as well as creating wealth for other people like me strictly by airing his approach and experiences. Did you know that the average millionaire goes bankrupt 3.5 times? And guess what—they're still millionaires, so even if it was real, who cares? Once you have acquired the knowledge and become a millionaire once, you just repeat the steps and you can be successful in any industry. Your uncle's bankruptcy filing is not the same; stop thinking small.

People hop from training course to training course, read all these books, and still have not tried to do anything. I can honestly say I have read maybe five paper books cover to cover since I graduated college. But I have listened to over two hundred audiobooks, maybe more, and sometimes the same ones over and over again. The advantage to audio is the ability to listen in the gym or while driving and maximize your time. Every single action I take is aligned with my goals.

In order for a high-quality mentor to invest their time in you, you need to be of value to them.

Picking a mentor needs to be based on how their accomplishments align with your core values. More often than not, people pay to be around these high-value mentors, to be in the same room with them and ask them questions, but then they end up not taking their advice. What the fuck are you doing? You've been handed a treasure map, only to say, "Oh, okay," and just put it down with all the other treasure maps you've collected throughout the years. Your learning needs to be active. Have faith in yourself and be ready to take action based on the advice you have received.

Aim to deeply understand your mentors and their motivators. If you are going to learn about someone, learn everything about them. Don't just recite one quote you saw online where they talk about compound interest. Compound interest is not going to make you a billionaire unless you want to wait till you are eighty and have hundreds of millions in cash to earn on.

MAKE IT MUTUALLY BENEFICIAL

In order for a high-quality mentor to invest their time in you, you need to be of value to them. Can you provide a service for them, take something off their plate, or serve as a connector for them? Figure out how you can help and lead with that. They are going to invest their time, money, thought, and energy in you if you show them you are valuable. Happy people practice gratitude, take care of themselves physically, and have strong connections. Good mentors are no different. They enjoy forming connections because they know what can be created through human capital.

A simple way to provide value to someone is to take their advice. People love to feel valued. I approach each interaction with no objective other than to listen and learn. The goal of having a mentor is to acquire their knowledge, so naturally their opinion is higher than mine on a scale of importance. However, this doesn't mean you can't do something to provide something of value to them.

You won't get far if you're looking for a free ride.

Think back to my example with Bob Mazer. After our initial interaction, I started going to him every time I came across a good deal. I provided him with the opportunity to make more money by acting as a connector. Now, when he has something to unload, he comes to me first. You won't get far if you're looking for a free ride. If you are taking, you are the equivalent of a drain, and a highly successful individual does not want to see their high-value knowledge go down a drain.

THE TAKER MENTALITY

I have a core group of real estate agents in my brokerage who have been with me since the start. Most of the agents who have left, believing that the grass was greener, have come back because they realized our in-house support services, like title and mortgage and our commission splits, are superior to other brokerages. I offer up to 95 percent commission splits. This split is unheard of. I do it for agents who give back and support the brokerage. I want everyone to win and am always willing to pay to make it happen.

As much as I love to give opportunity to people, I take issue with one group of people—the *takers*. These are the people who never call to ask how to grow their business or ask for advice but instead ask to have a fee waived, demand a discount, or request a raise. I would actually appreciate it if they instead asked, "How can I make more money?" That question shows me they want to do something to generate more revenue, not cut costs by asking for a raise on what they're already doing.

———

You would not have to ask for a pay raise if you were doing extraordinary work. Your company would notice.

———

Here is a tip for employees in any industry: You would not have to ask for a pay raise if you were doing extraordinary work. Your company would notice. So, if you haven't gotten a raise, I assure you there is something you're doing wrong.

CHAPTER 6

MASSIVE ACTION, MASSIVE HATE

Fun fact: losers hate winners. Strangers, friends, family . . . there are no exceptions. Get ready for a lot of "fuck yous" if you start massive contact marketing campaigns. Then after that, email them again! People will try to discourage you. Get used to it. It may be unintentional, like the time my mom told me I needed a job with a 401(k). It could be because they have given up, so they expect failure and try to get you to accept the sad reality of their wasted effort as a lesson to stay safe. It could be that they hate seeing people work. Either way, ignore it and understand that success is lonely. If the lavish lives you see on social media are real, behind them lie sleepless nights, countless hours of work, and unmeasurable effort.

Fun fact: losers hate winners. Strangers, friends, family . . . there are no exceptions.

People won't always like you, and most people are probably not happy to celebrate your wins. I'm fairly sure that half of our family who came to our housewarming party went back home saying all kinds of things about me, my wife, and our home. I even overheard someone calling our 9,000-square-foot home a "McMansion." To be clear, I don't call the house a mansion and never have. A McMansion is a cookie-cutter home built with shitty materials that stretches the borrower thin, not a hundred-year-old English manor with significant equity. This is one of the reasons I don't post personal things on social media. I don't want to invite hate into my life when it is already so abundant and close to home. You don't have to personally offend someone to make them dislike you. All you have to do is win. It is a phenomenon I don't understand; why hate someone who's successful? Wouldn't the better option be to show interest and learn from them?

Love me or hate me, at least you know me.

I am not offended if someone doesn't like me, and if you want to become a winner too, get ready to be criticized. Dislike should be a marker that you are doing something right because it means you have impacted someone so much that they think about you enough to form an opinion of you. Love me or hate me, at least you know me. My recruiters constantly tell me that agents know me from the thousands of emails I send. Their feelings toward my incessant emails are irrelevant at that point because if they're talking to my recruiter, it means we've made contact in person.

Every day is an opportunity to create the life you want.

I am driving toward a goal that I cannot be stopped from reaching, and other people are either beside me or behind me; people in my way are not tolerated, plain and simple. Every day is an opportunity to create the life you want. The word *character* originates from the Greek word *charassein*, which means to engrave, scratch, etch, or chisel. The more pain, struggle, and hate you suffer, the more your character becomes defined. Every decision you make chisels you into the person you will ultimately be. All repetitive behaviors create character, so repeat growth-driven behaviors if you want to be the best version of yourself. To find out what you are capable of, you have to put yourself out there and be ready to experience the hate, discouragement, and obstacles head-on. That is where you find your true character.

People who shield themselves from the negatives of growth are doing themselves a disservice. I find hate incredibly motivating because it comes from someone who could never be in your shoes and has no idea what they're talking about most of the time. How are you supposed to find out who is really on your side if you have blinders on? How are you supposed to push through the trenches if you're in denial of every negative thing that comes your way? Some of your friends and family are not clapping when you win, and that's okay. Acknowledge it and move on, but never be in denial.

Hate is a part of growth because it makes people uncomfortable to see others doing more than them.

Hate is a part of growth because it makes people uncomfortable to see others doing more than them. You are shifting the hierarchy by creating growth, especially if you're young. Hatred always comes from the bottom; no one ever punches down. If people speak negatively about others, they subconsciously believe the target of their unwanted opinion to be in an elevated hierarchical position compared to them. People who are not successful will do whatever they can to drag others down rather than lift themselves up. Ironically, the best way to elevate themselves is to learn from you, but they don't have the right mindset.

While I realize that hatred is not a pleasant experience, it is a necessary evil that weeds people out. This is especially important if you are working with others. When push comes to shove and you have to make tough decisions and have uncomfortable conversations that others don't want to have, watch your team to see how they behave. Do they vehemently oppose? Do they add more negativity to the situation? Get these people out of your way and out of your business. They won't help you make it.

In fact, they will usually get out of your way on their own. That is precisely what I have experienced with every bad partner and bad contractor who has joined SFG: they don't like how I operate, so they leave. Flight of the weak is something I don't have a problem with, and their opinion is something I don't give a second thought to because I wouldn't want to trade places with them. This is my life, and I will perform every necessary duty to advance it, including cutting loose ends.

People automatically think that you are a terrible person if you have money, which is crazy. I've had employees confront me and call me selfish and entitled. They don't realize that my goal is the success of my four hundred and fifty employees and their families. If they do well, I do well and vice versa. Instead of recognizing this, they jump to the conclusion that I'm brash and only focused on myself. Anyone who knows about growing a business knows this isn't true. My success is dependent on the success of the team. Don't allow others to project their insecurities, fears, and biases onto you.

When you get dead set on your goals and have a very clear picture of the kind of person you want to be, you will attract a certain caliber of people. Along with these like-minded individuals will come naysayers. Perception creates reality, and if you think of yourself as a winner, other people will too. Whatever personal feeling they develop from that is on them, not you. Take their gawking stares as a sign that you are moving in the right direction. People can say whatever they want to about me now, and it doesn't affect me at all. I don't let it upset me. I say fuck them and move on.

My wife has a problem with this bulletproof attitude, but she is used to it. At our house-warming party, we kept everything low-key, which sent her into a panic. She is a planner and likes to make a massive show of events. Naturally, she was worried about things beyond our control, like the weather and what everyone would think about the house, food, and so on. I was utterly unfazed. If they don't like the place, who cares? If they don't like the food, don't eat it. If they don't like the drink selection, don't drink it! They can leave just as quickly as they came. No one is holding a gun to their head. There is nothing wrong with wanting to have perfectly orches-trated events, but we often become focused on bad things like the opinions of others.

**A *no* today can turn into
a *yes* tomorrow.**

However, even after everything I have done, I still struggle with impostor syndrome, which I define as a feeling that you don't deserve to be in the room or at the table with ultrasuccessful people. I had butterflies in my stomach the whole way to Necker Island. There was this lingering self-doubt that the other attendees wouldn't see my value. Every one of them saw my worth, and they were impressed by it—likely a combination of the price I had paid for the event and my young age. Their reaction to me was great reinforcement, and that's why you should prioritize putting yourself in uncomfortable situations, because you are your own biggest enemy most of the time.

IT'S ALL ABOUT VOLUME

Never shy away from a challenge. Always prove to yourself and others that you have unwavering willpower. My brokerage just signed a top-producing agent that I have been messaging since 2016! Ironically, she still had all my messages and was impressed with my persistence. You cannot predict the future, but taking massive action makes things more likely to go in your favor. Stop worrying about what people think and focus on what volume and persistence can get you. A *no* today can turn into a *yes* tomorrow. Contact more people every day, over and over again. If you do that in any business, you inevitably win.

I've built my wealth in various industries, and I'm not intimidated by any industry. There will always be someone who knows more than you, but who cares? It's not hard to learn anything, and most information is free. If you're not putting yourself out there, you get nowhere. People worry about the most trivial things, which likely stems from insecurity or an ill-applied sense of self-importance. People love to think that everyone is thinking about them constantly. No one cares about your mistakes. For instance, I prioritize speed over typos—my message is still the same, and the most important thing is that it's getting delivered. I love when someone replies to one of my emails to tell me that I made a typo. I think it's so funny that they took the time to read the whole email, had enough presence of mind to find a typo, and then replied to me.

People fear calling a hundred people because they don't want to get turned down by ninety-nine. They never stop to think about the one person who would have said *yes*. Not taking action will never get you a *yes*. A large portion of success can be boiled down to creating volume. Making one hundred phone calls every day with a 1 percent capture rate doesn't sound insane when you think about the long-term results. One hundred calls can turn into one listing a day if you're a real estate agent.

Set yourself up for success by creating the right mindset. Decide that you will push on, even when people hang up on you. Keep moving on to the next one and the next, and so on, until you hit your daily goal. There should be no personal emotion tied to your action except for an insatiable hunger to hit your goals. Don't take a *no* personally. Just call them again tomorrow and again the following week. Maybe you did not provide them enough value the first time. Say, "If I'm working this hard now, imagine how hard I'll work if I work with you." Let your actions communicate this to them.

When you grow, you will start to notice a shift in the attitudes of those around you. Dealing with this has to be a part of the plan. Shifting your mindset to that of a winner is key. Instead of focusing on how you can fail, focus only on how you can win. Winners play the long game; they worry about winning the championship instead of focusing on each individual game. That mindset makes a huge difference in how you play every day. It has been proven that people with well-defined goals do better. Look it up. Make it your obligation to hit your goals, sell yourself, and create the life you want. Create a space of resilience by believing in yourself and what you are selling. And make yourself invincible.

CHAPTER 7

NO SUCH THING AS WORK-LIFE BALANCE

There's no such thing as work-life balance. Not if you want to do anything great, at least. Extreme success is the product of an unsatiated hunger, a hunger that requires zero balance and a willingness to do whatever it takes. As an entrepreneur, you have to rank everything on a scale of importance as it relates to your purpose. Dinner with friends: not important. Dinner with a potential client or agent: very important. Your friends will likely be upset by this, but they would get over it if they had your best interest in mind. Better yet, if they had enough going on, they wouldn't be available for dinner either. Your plans outside of those aimed at achieving need to remain fluid, and you have to understand that your life will not be in balance, at least not for a while. I never could have grown SFG to a company with over four hundred employees and independent contractors without years of sixteen-to-eighteen hour workdays, which included an array of bullshit like playing janitor, housekeeper, teacher, administrator, and so on.

Balance creates a void, an empty slot in your day that allows you to waste time on activities that do not *create*. Growth takes constant creation. It does not make sense to seek balance, thus emptiness, before you have created greatness.

The pursuit of this false ideal is exacerbated by mediocre societal standards and self-help books that tell you to do less because they know this is the messaging that people want to hear. Who wouldn't want to hear that they should stay home and do nothing more often?

Set your immediate feelings aside and become laser-focused on the life you envision for yourself.

This is not my messaging; I promote seeking balance in the long term by creating daily chaos now. Create the freedom to do whatever you want by sacrificing your time and feelings right now. Work-life balance is a lie that sounds nice and gets you nothing. Good things do not come to those who wait; they come to those who work.

Set your immediate feelings aside and become laser-focused on the life you envision for yourself. I don't care about how I feel waking up at 7:30 a.m. every morning. It's irrelevant because grinding every day gets deals done and makes me money. What's not to love about that? Where would I be if I told prospective agents that Sundays are my rest days and I can't meet? Take a guess. Greatness is created in extremes; balance is the absence of extremes.

Every day you are alive is a day that is knocked off your lifespan. There is no time to stop and smell the roses, so allow your work to create the roses. Fall in love with what you can create. I love what I'm doing, not the industry, which is something I've said over and over again. I'm in love with the rewards of constantly grinding.

Look at it this way: if your goal is to be a fantastic parent, do you limit your involvement to a set number of hours per week? Hell, no! If you want to be a great parent, you must be committed to it 24/7. Where's the balance there? It is no different than being driven and focused on growing yourself and your business.

WORK-LIFE BALANCE LIMITS YOU

Is there even such a thing as a work-life balance? The concept doesn't make any sense. Do you really feel balanced if you are making time to relax and miss it, or if you spend all day in bed and neglect your to-do list? Isn't ensuring your financial freedom and not being a burden to your family more rewarding than making time to watch two hours of TV daily? People who seek work-life balance achieve nothing because balance does not exist in a world of greatness.

Never forget that opportunities don't come your way based on your schedule. Opportunities don't look at your schedule, see when you have an opening, and decide to leap at you. They are like small floaters in your peripheral vision waiting for you to capture them. You need to make those phone calls and go to those meetings when they come up because if you don't, you will lose out. Become an expert at using every second of every day, and leverage your time wisely.

Instead of trying to achieve work-life balance, ask yourself what your life is lacking and make it a goal to achieve that. The pillars of your ideal life should include excess in relationships, spiritual connectivity, health, and wealth. *Excess*, not *balance*. Are you seeking balance because you are burned out, because you don't have huge goals, or because you are just not hungry enough? I doubt it is because you want to let yourself down and lead a mediocre life. Your life will get filled with bullshit no matter how much balance you try to maintain. Make shit happen instead of letting the meaningless bullshit take over. I don't understand how people try to learn about passive income when they have yet to create stable active income.

The craziest thing is that you don't even have to start out being good at what you are doing; you just need to keep doing it over and over again. I hired replacements for myself for each separate SFG entity so they could duplicate what I was doing while I was still doing it. I achieve balance by maximizing my potential, a balance I define as prioritizing and executing on things that need to get done at that time and going all-in. Clocking in nine-to-five is not balance; it is average. Seek clarity of purpose. Clarity is what will push you to keep working, keep calling, keep moving, and keep taking action. Your priorities will change as you grow. That is okay as long as your priorities are aligned with your purpose.

LEVERAGE YOUR TIME

Successful people work until the task is done, not until the clock strikes a particular hour. Control your destiny by controlling every second of every day. My goal of building SFG into a company that does $100 million in revenue requires that I utilize every available second and every available resource.

My wife is a nurse practitioner candidate currently in grad school. I love it when her calendar is filled with clinicals, class, and work. Sometimes she has only two days off a month and is always gone from either 7:00 a.m. to 5:00 p.m. or 7:00 a.m. to 7:00 p.m. That is impressive! I'm not the kind of husband who will complain about not seeing my wife; she is working, and I love her more for it. We would hate it if we were off for a whole week and at home. There is nothing impressive about that to me.

If you want to gauge your income, take a look at your schedule. If you have huge gaps of free time, then you are wasting time. Stop finding excuses and fill that time with productive things that get you closer to your goals. Mapping out your schedule directly correlates to mapping out your action potential.

One of the first things I do when I meet with someone who is not performing well is ask them to take out their phones and check their screen time. This is an excellent tool to gauge your productivity. Maybe if you didn't average three hours a day on social media for the past few weeks, your productivity wouldn't be so low. What good is social media going to do when you're looking at some guy on a jet and you end up feeling envious of his life?

Mapping out your schedule directly correlates to mapping out your action potential.

What you don't think about when looking at that guy on the jet is all the massive action he took to *get* that jet. Another thing you likely don't think about is the reasoning behind using the jet: it saves time. A jet is not just a pretty object; it creates freedom. It's why I bought a plane and got my pilot's license. I own property in Pittsburgh, so instead of driving five hours for a meeting, I can fly there in an hour and a half and come back the same day.

Any way you can multiply your time is well worth it. If you are focused on growth, your priority should be maximizing all capital available. Most of us start with human capital as our only capital (more on that later). If you start off broke as I did, it's imperative to leverage your time, skills, and willpower. Most of your problems are self-inflicted because you choose to flounder around helplessly and pretend that the universe is against you instead of just getting to work.

I didn't hire a chief of operations to free myself up for wasting time; I hired one so I could free myself up to get more shit done. I utilized my human capital to create financial capital to acquire more human capital. Now someone else does everything I used to do while I am busy focusing on growth in other areas, not fucking off. SFG is so big that I need multiple people to handle its daily operations. There would be no way to scale each of the businesses if my daily involvement were necessary. If an acquisition is made or a problem arises, I am elbow-deep in problem-solving mode; this would make other areas suffer if operations depended solely on me.

I have ensured that my companies are adequately maintained by implanting people who perform my functions. This is the correct way to achieve balance and multiply productivity. Work your ass off and hire people to do what you do so you can do other things. This allows balance to be a reward based on performance, and this should be the only version of balance in your life.

YOU ARE YOUR BIGGEST PROBLEM

People like to focus on the *how* and not the *what* or *why*. Instead of repeatedly asking yourself *how*, ask yourself *what* you want and *why* you want it. If you're constantly focused and your vision is clear, how you make it happen becomes less relevant. A clear vision is a driver as powerful as the biological need to breathe. You don't think about breathing. You just do it.

Imagine you're a gas-powered machine, push the pedal all the way down, and take off full-force. Saying you want work-life balance is akin to telling the universe to pass you over for opportunities. Big moves need to be constantly happening. Seek growth over balance. There is no secret sauce to success; it takes years of dedication and hard work.

For some reason, working hard has become a bad thing in our culture; it used to be something that impressed people. This messaging comes from a society with social welfare systems that reward people for staying at home and doing nothing while at the same time penalizing people for working too much. The point is that we are being trained to be lazy, implicit, unquestioning underachievers. I don't know about you, but I'd rather work every hour of every day for something

I have control over instead of clocking in for forty hours and placing my future in someone else's hands.

EXCEL AT EVERYTHING

Allow this to put things into perspective: the most money I ever made as an employee was $7.40 an hour at Pep Boys when I was sixteen years old. I was a service advisor, or customer service rep, so my job was to work the register, work the floor, and sign people up for maintenance, among other things. They wouldn't pay me overtime, and besides, time-and-a-half of $7.40 would still have kept me broke.

There is no secret sauce to success; it takes years of dedication and hard work.

They had a commission structure for their salespeople, which I soon realized was the only way I could make extra money. I managed to make over $1,000 a week most of the time. How? Because I dedicated every second I was there to getting the job done and pushing my agenda. I was selling everything and working every chance I got. My coworkers hated me, but I was there to make money, not friends. I was getting ready to start college and knew I wouldn't make a career out of Pep Boys, but I still had something to prove and money to make.

The most uncomfortable part of selling is introducing the sale while avoiding the dreaded "Would you like anything else today?" Once I got comfortable with the products I was selling and with my customer base, the interactions became easier. People didn't suspect a sixteen-year-old kid was tugging at their wallets, and I took advantage of that. I even started watching the mechanics and learned how to do oil changes. Eventually, I started asking them to show me how to do certain things, and the next thing you know, I was cranking out oil changes.

I created a win-win situation for the mechanics and myself because I could take a few jobs off of their plates. This also made me more knowl-edgeable, thus making it easier for me to sell. The position you're in is irrelevant if you're disciplined and dedicated. I was a minimum-wage worker at Pep Boys, but I made thousands of dollars and learned valuable skills. You are an economy of one, and it is always up to you to put yourself out there and stand out above the rest. Stop waiting for things to come to you and worrying about what others can do for you. Do for *yourself*.

CHAPTER 8

BUILD A REAL BUSINESS

t's time to face the facts: having an LLC or selling things on an e-commerce platform doesn't make you an entrepreneur. An entrepreneur takes risks and is focused on scaling their business. There are so many people on the Internet pandering about how they are incredibly successful entrepreneurs. The truth is likely that they have never made a million dollars, and their business is getting you to buy their motivational course. If you really wanted to learn how to do something, you would just fucking Google it.

Money cannot be made passively until it is worked for and earned.

The four-day workweek and the balance they are selling sound nice, but they don't get results! I am a millionaire, and I still work seven days a week. I don't understand why people think they deserve things without working for them. Money cannot be made passively until it is worked for and earned, so get over it.

The reality is that you do not have a real company if you are not selling, producing, or providing a service that you can scale. Even people who make revenue on one-time products, like the guy who created the copper sleeve and now makes $50 million a year on revenue due to his product being acquired by a major company, once had to work day and night to develop his product. You can have a great exit, but you have to make something worth acquiring first.

Being an entrepreneur has nothing to do with not reporting to anyone. I hate that the notion of "being your own boss" is propagated as entrepreneurship. As the head of SFG, I have more than four hundred people to answer to. Your employees, your customers, your family, and yourself—those are all people you have to answer to, people who depend on you. If you attempt to gain flexibility and loosen your responsibility, you don't want to be an entrepreneur; you want to be a bum.

You can have a great exit, but you have to make something worth acquiring first.

Don't start anything if you don't have a clear idea of what it will require you to sacrifice. You'll just waste your time and fail. I report to my people like they are all CEOs because I will hear about it if I can't make payroll, and my agents will leave if I do not provide value, period. Becoming a business owner is not about not reporting to people. It is probably the most significant test of accountability you will ever encounter.

Having more than four hundred families that I impact financially definitely keeps me up at night. That's what a business is—something that provides value. Your employees depend on you to pay them competitively for their work, health benefits, growth, and so much more. My people are very loyal to me because they know what I offer them, and I always deliver. I have forgone quarterly disbursements so that I can pay my shareholders instead. That is how much I care about running a company and keeping my company running. I am here for growth, and I let the money follow.

Technically, if you are a solopreneur, you are selling yourself. If you create replicable systems and processes, you can make a killing. However, to replicate, you need to grow. You can be the point of origin, but you need to develop multiple means of delivery. The concept of a solopreneur is a strange one, and it's eaten up by people who don't want to work. Entrepreneurs with employees exchange money for time, and solopreneurs and freelancers trade time for money, just like an employee.

Earlier, I mentioned that 20 percent of the 31.7 million small businesses in America are run by solopreneurs who don't even have one employee. Profitable companies operating above a 20–25 percent margin make $250,000+ per employee. Companies that make less than $85,000 per employee operate at almost zero margin. Our title company averages $363,000 a year per employee in gross revenue. If you want to exceed that number, you need to perform and find other people who can perform.

Other people can be hired to solve your problems, so use them. Make each addition seamless by having replicable systems and processes—that is, the same onboarding process, training programs, and metric trackers. Don't be scared to get rid of people as you build your company; the right team is imperative. You also need to get the right leader to ensure that every new addition exceeds expectations. In the beginning, you may have to function as leadership yourself to make sure every new addition is exceeding expectations. However, after enough perseverance, you can hire that role away too.

In the business world and real estate world, many people believe that it's all on them to succeed. This is technically true, but if you figure out a way to dissect your ideas and transform them into a system, like standard operating procedures, your mission can be outsourced and scaled by hiring more people; this creates an exponential growth factor in your business. Even if you don't sell the business, simply having your philosophy in place and replicated will drum up more business.

BORN RICH

I struggled when deciding to add this section. I thought it had nothing to do with my get-off-your-ass-and-get-to-work strategy for making money. After all, people who are born rich or inherit a large amount of wealth don't have to work for it. They ride on the coattails of the moneymakers before them. But here's the thing about inheriting wealth: you can't make it last without knowing what to do with it.

Think of the lottery winners and professional athletes who have it all, then lose everything because of their shitty spending habits. I know this sounds far-fetched, but people born into wealth have their own sets of problems. If you're born at the top, you still have to work to stay at the top. The stats are against these people; 70 percent of wealthy families lose their wealth by the second generation. Inheritors of wealth need to learn about managing, reinvesting, and rein-venting their wealth.

A full pot doesn't stay full forever if it's constantly getting tapped and never refilled. I cannot stress the importance of teaching your heirs about money management and frugality. My kids will be flying coach. I can afford first class; they cannot. I refuse to have *daddy's money* kids. I want resilient, self-reliant problem solvers.

A full pot doesn't stay full forever if it's constantly getting tapped and never refilled.

Don't allow your kids to be blind to tough financial decisions. I'm not saying you should tell your kids about the sleepless nights, bad deals, nonperforming partners, lawsuits, or breached contracts. But they should understand that hard work is a necessary element of achievement and that money is a tool that can be played with strategically to create expansion. Encourage kids to create their own achievement so they don't fall into a purgatory created by nonperformance and shitty decisions.

JACK-OF-ALL-TRADES, MASTER OF NONE

The biggest mistake anyone can make is being a jack-of-all-trades and putting everything on themselves or not trusting other people. There's a belief in the beginning that you have to play every role. This keeps you small and preoccupied with menial bullshit. Get away from that as quickly as you can and reinvest the money you are making into staff! Hire away your weaknesses; don't waste time learning new skills. If you adopt the philosophy of hiring fast and firing fast, you quickly weed out ill-fitting people and can build a team of the right people. You absolutely should weed out weak links; if you're paying someone $75,000 a year and they aren't hitting the goals you want them to hit, they are stealing your money. Get them out of the way so you can reallocate your funds to those who are going to produce results.

It doesn't take much time to figure out if a person is a weak link. If you don't get the right vibe in an interview, thank them for coming and move on to the next person, plain and simple. The company and revenue need to come first; nothing else should be considered. This is a concept of hierarchy that many people can't understand. Employees are essential, but the company's success is even more critical because you would not have employees or be able to pay the employees without the company.

By keeping someone on board who is not good at their job, you're doing the company, everyone at the company (including yourself), and the employee a disservice. Case in point: I had to fire an employee whom I liked very much. The problem was that she became overwhelmed easily and literally cried every time someone asked her to do something outside of her regular duties or if she felt like she had done something wrong. It made other employees uncomfortable and hurt productivity. It didn't matter how much

I liked her. I couldn't continue to spend money to employ her because she was not serving the company to the best of her abilities.

To lie to this person and let them keep their job even though they were underperforming would be a disservice to them as fellow humans. Some people are doing a shitty job, and they should be made aware of it so they can stop. I even had to fire one of my admins at RE/MAX who had become a friend. It was a no-brainer to replace her with someone more experienced who was also an accountant. The admin we fired had less experience and also brought along a lot of baggage. I noticed I had started staying away from the office because she was always so negative.

This negative admin was responsible for paying the agents and being the face of the business. Negativity spreads like wildfire, so the agents would be negative if she was negative. People in the office would talk about it, and I started getting complaints. I knew if it went unchecked, the brokerage would lose people. I fired her in the morning, right before the workday began, because I wanted people to see her packing up.

Naturally, she was upset, but it allowed me to redefine the direction of the brokerage and highlight the ideal candidate while simultaneously letting everyone know I wasn't taking any shit. Everyone already knew she was a negative underperformer, so keeping her would have given the wrong message. Believe it or not, a public firing sometimes goes well, almost like a public execution, but let's not get that carried away. My expectations became apparent, and I sent the message: get with it or get out, and if you don't remove yourself, I have no trouble doing it for you. My business needs everyone to be on the same page, and one person can completely shift company culture.

THE TRUE MEANING OF LOYALTY

Be loyal to yourself and your vision. Before making additions to your company, you have to define your expectations and organizational culture standards clearly. The starting place is your ethics and values, which will ultimately determine the direction of the entire organization. If you still haven't secured a mentor, had a mindset shift, established a routine, curated a vision, and started working ten times harder than a billionaire building a company, stop here and go back. Again, your values will define the organization, so if you're still frazzled and losing your keys, you won't be able to develop a culture of growth.

It's the law of attraction: people weed themselves out if the organizational culture is clearly defined with strict accountability measures. Unlike most people, I love it when people exit my life and business. Not because I'm ruthless or get some sick delight out of it—that would be weird and cruel. I love it because it means that I am doing an excellent job building my company's culture. People sense this and exit if they disagree, which creates less work for my management team and me. I run a top-down company and always lead by example. I want you to be on time, so I'm always on time. I am always conscious of what people think I believe is important.

Even when I make additions, I am very conscious to choose individuals who have similar outlooks to me before I train it into them. It took me a year and a half to find a COO, and it was worth the wait because I was able to secure someone who was leaving the military as a Green Beret major. We work well together because we have similar values, ethics, and morals. He is someone

I know will consistently reflect the organizational culture I have built, whether or not I'm there. The goal is to create constant reinforcement of the same ideals which trickle down into the company.

JUST COMMIT

I recently made a massive investment in coaching: I bought a large number of spots for a proven coaching platform shown to increase earnings up to 40 percent. I rolled this opportunity out to everyone in the company across all industries on a first-come, first-served basis. The only catch was that they had to send $200 by the end of the week to receive log-in credentials. I promised to double their initial investment if they attended every session of the month-long program. There were two hundred people on the initial call, about sixty people who emailed to tell me that they would send me the money by the end of the day, and only twenty-nine people who actually sent in the $200.

I received several payments and emails after the cutoff time asking about sign-up. Their money was sent back, none were offered the program, and they learned a lesson in commitment. If you can't even commit to something that will help you produce more and make a couple of hundred bucks just by tuning in, then you don't want to make more money, plain and simple.

What can you commit to if you can't even commit to making more money and creating freedom for yourself? Your spouse, kids, business associates, and friends should all be scared of you. Someone who is not driving forward is holding themselves, and everyone who associates with them, back. Committing $200 to growth and even just to get an extra $200 back was too much for the people who passed up on the offered opportunity. At this point, there is nothing more I can do for these people.

Offering opportunities, sitting back, and watching people flounder is an excellent way to identify those who lack commitment. If your employees or business associates cannot commit to themselves, they will never be able to commit to you or your company. This is a testament to how a solid company culture can help you. A great culture offers passive tests that ultimately allow people to reveal themselves and their intentions. As a boss, you no longer have to hawk every move, which saves you time and stress.

AVOID STAYING SMALL

Newsflash: if you were good at your side hustle, it wouldn't be a side hustle. Lose your pride and start changing the things that need to change in order for you to grow. Ego, lack of vision, lack of trust in others, and a lack of fundamental processes in place are a few reasons that come to mind when I think about people who keep their small businesses small.

Ego happens to be one of the biggest problems I have encountered in real estate. No one wants anyone to tell them what to do, and no one accepts advice. The only thing this means is that ego is getting in the way of receiving help and propelling your business. Yes, it's your business. You filed the LLC, but who cares if your business is not doing business? Learn to take advice from people who have been there and done that. Your pride and ego will get you nothing, especially when they are unwarranted. A billionaire earned their ego, but an agent doing six deals a year . . . not so much. Look, I'm not knocking the little guy; I'm knocking the guy who stays small because they get in their own way.

Ask yourself this: What does a side hustle even mean? If you are not interested in building a real company that does real business and is continually focused on growth, why are you even wasting your time? To call yourself an entrepreneur? To feed your ego? If you can make more money doing overtime at your real job, your side hustle is a hobby, and you should reevaluate your priorities. If you are focused on growing your business, the process does everything *but* feed your ego. It's draining. It's discouraging. It's all-consuming. I do it because I don't have a choice. My last "real" job was at Pep Boys. Do you think I'm going back there? Hell, no!

No matter how you invest your time, money, and energy, the point of an investment is growth.

No matter how you invest your time, money, and energy, the point of an investment is growth. I don't go to the gym six days a week with the hopes of becoming an unhealthy fat fuck. Until you decide to focus full-time, you will be wasting your time. My brother has two nutrition stores in New Jersey, and for a while he was trying to sell real estate at the same time. Seriously, why?

There was no point—his stores are killing it, and his number-one priority should be to continue to kill it. Hurting the thing he was good at to make an extra $6,000 a year on one real estate deal was not worth it. Over time, going all-in and growing his nutrition stores will pay off tenfold.

Instead of trying to dip your hands into everything, make one thing pay off exponentially and move on when the payout buys you freedom.

CHAPTER 9

DECENTRALIZED COMMAND

Think delegation, but bigger. A decentralized command is an approach to delegation that reaches into every facet of your life. Don't waste time doing anything that someone else can do for you.

I don't mow my lawn, I don't do the grocery shopping (neither does my wife), and we don't clean our house anymore. I cut back on menial tasks long before I started making actual money. Why? Because these things take away the only thing that generates revenue for me: my time.

If you are a solopreneur, how much more money could you make by delegating simple tasks? Working harder than others increases the time you have available for productivity; not filling your day with stupid bullshit *also* increases the time you have available for productivity.

If you are working at the same pace as someone else, both of you are killing it—making calls, networking, meeting people. The only difference is, the other guy still does their cleaning (four hours a week), their grocery shopping (two hours a week), their cooking (five hours a week), and all of that other necessary junk that eats away at their time, but you don't. You hired housekeepers for $50, paid an extra $5 for grocery delivery, and used a meal prep service. You just bought yourself eleven hours a week, forty-four hours a month, or over five hundred hours a year—the equivalent to twelve extra forty-hour workweeks. The other guys are putting in forty-hour workweeks, but you are creating an *extra* workweek every month. The sheer volume of this work ethic will inevitably beat out the other guy. It's simple: doing more gets more done.

Stop doing your own taxes, stop managing your social media accounts, stop doing anything not directly connected to making money or your goal. Why do you need to do your taxes online? It's risky, and there are tons of chances you will mess it up and get audited. Then what? You fucked yourself over by shining a microscope on yourself and your financials.

If you scale your business, you will need to bring in an accounting firm eventually, so save yourself time, money, and risks and do it now.

I have no business spending twelve hours building a website, and even if I did, it would probably be shitty because that's not what I do. Get someone else who knows what they're doing to do it. The only thing I have on my phone for social media is the Facebook ads manager. I check it once a week to see how things are going, and I don't dig any deeper.

I lead from the front and trust my team to accomplish tasks, but I am always ready to jump in if needed because I free myself of unnecessary tasks. You must maintain unity of command always. A business's profitability is heavily dependent on its operational efficiency. I don't let things slide, and I always make sure everyone is operating at peak performance levels.

WADING THROUGH MURKY WATER

I've said it before, and I'll say it again: I thrive in chaos. An effective CEO should thrive in creating chaos. What is chaos? Constant creation: creation of ideas, projects, and new problems. Creation drives revenue. I love feeling like I'm drowning in my to-do list; I want more problems, and even bigger ones. Growth is made possible through delegation. I couldn't have the wherewithal to continue creating if I still had to worry about my business's everyday ins and outs. You might say, "But Joe, I'm still growing my business, and I can't afford to hire someone right now." To that, I say, make more money. Work harder, create more, and don't be scared to spend the money on something or someone who will free you up to do more moneymaking.

If you've not yet been able to surmise my concept of freedom, it is freedom from constraints, freedom to do more and be more. If you still think freedom means you get to do nothing, just put this book down and get back to doing nothing. No one can help you, because you don't want to help yourself.

> **To delegate effectively, you have to make sure people understand your intent and their roles within the organization.**

If my people are calling me to double-check every single transaction they make, then I might as well do it myself. More time is wasted accepting the phone call and listening to an explanation.

Delegation often fails because of poorly defined standard operating procedures and leadership roles and expectations. To delegate effectively, you have to make sure people understand your intent and their roles within the organization. There has to be a method to the madness. In the military, we refer to this as the *commander's intent*. There is a clear, specific mission for everyone on the team, and everyone has individual roles they need to own. My executives are building handbooks explaining their roles and associated tasks, making replication and expansion of the management team easier. This means it can occur without my involvement or the hiring team getting bogged down by the details of a key new hire. At the same time, I have all W-2 employees making a handbook of their own daily responsibilities. It is an exercise that makes employees think about what their roles are, identify any overlap, and it helps us uncover employees who are underutilized or just plain confused. This ultimately allows me to cut costs, retrain, and redefine roles within the organization.

IT HAS TO BE DONE NOW FOR A REASON

What I do in a day sometimes feels like what most people do in a month, and because I have so much to do, I prioritize speed and addressing things right away. If someone does something wrong, I want to address it immediately rather than wait for the sales meeting at the end of the month to bring it up publicly. There is no need to involve two hundred people who are not involved because someone was too afraid to talk to someone directly.

As the company has grown, many of my responsibilities have shifted to members of management. It is incredibly frustrating to have ineffective leaders who are afraid of conflict and wait to address things until it's too late. If this happens, it is an immediate red flag for me, and I know this manager either needs to be retrained or does not have a place on my team. It is never okay to wait to address a problem. Like an infection or a parasite, the issue will grow and continue to spread if not immediately stopped.

Making fast decisions speeds everything up and keeps the momentum alive. Remember that *not* making a decision is still a decision. Being slow to act will slow your plans and delay your goals. It will also weigh on you and likely add more stress than if you had just pulled the trigger when first presented with the opportunity. It's like when you're taking a test: your first answer is most likely the correct answer. Think of your mind as a flowing river and the decisions you're putting off as blockages in the river. The more things you put off, the bigger the backup becomes, and ultimately the outflow is decreased.

There is no need to overanalyze. It's a waste of time; things will get figured out as they happen. I have personally never written down a business plan, and in fact, I didn't start writing down my goals until I started following Grant Cardone. But I still will not write down a business plan. If a bank asks me to write a business plan to get a loan, I will go to another bank. Why would you spend time writing a business plan that will change? Action gets things done, not planning.

Your personality type and presets are your responsibility to identify and mitigate

---

The coaching company I hired made us all take the DiSC personality assessment, and one of the women who runs operations is the complete opposite of me. She was asked to name one thing that I could do better. She said, "Well, that is a really tough question because I have known Joe for seven years. But he has the most unrealistic timelines. That could be better, except then we wouldn't be here right now without his 'act-fast, think-fast, no-excuses' mentality."

The point of mentioning this? Your personality type and presets are your responsibility to identify and mitigate; they're not for you to live by and use as a pool of excuses. I don't care what your personality type is; I care that you can be introspective and identify your weaknesses. This person is the complete opposite of me, but she still gets shit done.

CHAPTER 10

HUMAN CAPITAL

What got you here won't take you to the next level. Every time you hit a new level, you evolve and become someone new. Once that happens, forget about how you made it before and get ready to do something different to keep the climb going. A lot of people assume that growth is a straight upward line. Yet once you begin to elevate, you find yourself doing things you never even thought were possible. I still network, except now, I've hired company representation to go to industry mixers, and I network on private islands. The goal is the same, but the means and levels of achievement are different.

The not-so-secret secret to my success is human capital. Human capital is an intangible asset not listed on a company's balance sheet. Human capital includes all your experience, skills, network, and everything you are willing to do to get what you want. It also consists of the individuals you choose to add to your network and company. We've already covered this, and by now, you know that all labor is not created equal, so choose wisely.

Human capital is SFG's most important asset because everything we do is service-based. The people are the company. They are maintaining the systems, performing operations, and driving revenue. It is vital that they be fully equipped to handle every challenge thrown at them. While I'm not a good coach, I am good at identifying the qualities I lack and hiring them away.

I *am* good at getting things done though. If someone comes to me with a problem, I solve the problem; that's it! I'm not going to talk to them about it. I'm not good at communicating with people, and sometimes I can be blunt or even blow people off. What I can do is solve their problems—that's my version of empathy. I am task-oriented and effective. That may not be your style. It's your job to find your own style and supplement the areas where you are lacking.

If you haven't already found your DiSC personality type, I highly suggest making that a starting point. Identify your weaknesses and hire them away. I know what I'm good at, what I suck at, what I don't like to do, and so on. I hire people who can fill my gaps. I may not want to have small talk about someone's day or family, but I take my duty to produce and sustain families very seriously. This is something people find so hard to understand, so instead of arguing my point to everyone who complains about me, I hired a manager who can have the small talk and build a community.

Now that the company is doing $30 million in revenue across the board and constantly bringing on new acquisitions, I no longer have the capacity to handle all of it and still be the visionary. I can't give them the coaching and attention they need. Do I give up and say, "Okay, that's enough growth for now," and hit the pause button, or do I continue growing by utilizing other talented people? The answer is clear.

When I was looking for a chief of operations, I said I needed a guy who has managed way more people than I have. My guy managed over four hundred soldiers, $100 million in assets, and $50 million in cash. He is a great coach and a seasoned leader.

HIRE THE RIGHT PROFESSIONALS

When you start a business or project, you play every role, even those you may be terrible at. Don't take things slow; growth is a race, and you will need to add people to your team to get to the next level. You have to realize that a one-person show is not enough to make change. I create the culture, drive the workload, and provide the support, but the team ensures every note is hit on the head. My team is going to take the company to the next level.

Never turn your back on others because you are small-minded, selfish, or a know-it-all. Creating alliances and partnerships is what has allowed me to grow. Real estate agents are independent contractors, free to come and go as they please. The culture and support that my brokerage provides are what attract them and make them stay. Never underestimate the power of making yourself attractive and valuable to others.

People are egotistical, but forming necessary partnerships requires you to drop your pride. You can be the most driven person in the world, but if you can't sell yourself or your product, you won't get very far. Conquering the sea requires multiple captains and multiple ships. You have to deal with other captains on the voyage you are planning. Once you think of it this way, you realize that you are also a product to be sold. You need other people, particularly other captains, to buy into your vision. These captains will serve as your company leadership.

Learn to trust. You cannot be present on every ship. Hire the right individuals who you are

confident will execute your vision. I am a noto-
rious blind truster. I don't have time to waste
months babysitting someone before giving them
large tasks to handle. I thoroughly vet new hires,
and if they continually disappoint me, I don't keep
them around. I expect competence at the outset,
not after an arbitrary probationary period.

Employment at SFG is performance-based.
Don't waste your money paying someone who
is not performing. Cut your losses and move on
quickly. Hire professionals who not only fit the job
description but who also align with your vision for
your business and company culture. Professionals
deserve autonomy . . . until they don't.

To create an organization that thrives, you need
the right players. The right employees and the right
attorneys, accountants, and consultants mesh with
your business goals and philosophy. This may be
harder than it sounds, considering that many of
these professionals focus on minutiae and may not
be able to see your big picture. Always remember
your vision, your company, and your rules. These
professionals are not business owners or risk-
takers; they are employees at companies who are
comfortable with their salaries.

I tend to separate everyone into two cate-
gories: risk-takers and non-risk-takers. Not

everyone is a risk-taker, and that is okay—but I would never allow anyone who is not a risk-taker to give me business advice. Hired professionals are hired to do their jobs; I want my accountant to run the numbers, not tell me how to interpret the results. My CFO's only job is to make sure the numbers are right and to tell me what my money looks like, not how to spend it. These people don't have the risk tolerance or drive you do, and they won't be able to see the playing field the way an entrepreneur would. Appreciate and respect their expertise, but stay wary.

SUPPORT SERVICE PROVIDERS

I was taught by a mentor that if your support professionals start giving you business advice, ask them these three questions:

1. How many employees do you currently have?
2. Have you ever owned a company?
3. What is the largest exit you have ever had?

If they cannot answer these questions, they have no business telling you how to run your business.

Support services are expensive! Utilize them appropriately, and never let someone take control from you. Attorneys are good for four things: business structuring, filing paperwork for lawsuits, litigation, and their error and omissions insurance so I can sue them if something goes wrong. The point is that most are not worth their billable hours—especially if they're spending your money on hours of advising you on something they have never done themselves.

I fired an accountant recently from one of the top firms in the country. They sent tax services bills and included a charge for their research to find out if I could write off expenses related to my airplane. How ridiculous that I should be expected to pay for an expert's research. It's unacceptable. I expect an expert to know the ins and outs of their specialty, and if they don't, at a minimum, I should not be charged for their lack of experience/expertise. Service providers should be treated as employees; their funding is conditional on their performance. Nonperformance is theft.

You work hard to be able to pay people for their services. Don't let them steal your time and money.

CHAPTER 11

YOU DON'T NEED TO LOVE THE WORK

People always ask me *how*. How have I gone from being a realtor to this? I just fucking work harder than anyone I know. I don't have a secret recipe, and I don't believe in balance. I believe in creating a vision for your life and going after it full-force, obliterating any obstacles that get in your way even when it's your self-righteousness that has created those obstacles. Your vision comes first, always with no exceptions. You have to be able to step outside of your micro view of the world and see everything with macroscopic tunnel vision explicitly curated to reach your goals. You have to be hungry enough to stop doing everything that does not serve your purpose and wise enough to understand everything that needs to be set in motion to accomplish your goals.

What is your game plan? Mine is constantly fueled by biting off more than I can chew, committing first, and figuring out the rest when I need to. I surround myself with people who are bigger than me and soak up their advice as if my life depended on it. Every opportunity is a learning opportunity, and I make conscious consumption decisions about everything in my life, including people and the media and books I consume. I never let bullshit take up my time, never celebrate small wins, never dwell on losses, and stay committed to working hard, especially when I reach a pinnacle. There is no end point unless you tell yourself there is one. I am committed to growing, succeeding, and being the biggest player out there.

I never viewed hard work or accomplishments as a means to receiving a trophy or praise. I work hard because it is my only option. I have big goals, and they require action every day. I don't love the work; I love the possibilities of freedom that working hard provides.

Name five people off the top of your head who would say they enjoy making calls for eight or more hours every day. I bet you can't. Hell, I wouldn't say I like working out every day, but the alternative is worse. The pursuit of the goal or the purpose is what you need to look forward to most. Don't get bogged down by the details; stay focused on the big picture. You can find fun in anything as long as you have purpose driving you forward.

Take an example from the military: I don't think anyone enjoys getting shot at or the possibility of being blown to pieces. They are willing to go overseas and sacrifice their freedoms and liberties to ensure those same freedoms and liberties for everyone they know. There is pride in being a patriot and protecting one's country. That's what motivates people to join the military.

If you love what you do, you will never work a day in your life. Bullshit. Work is always work. Even a bartender at a beach bar in Costa Rica has shitty days. What you are doing now doesn't matter as much as what you are working toward. I have always wanted to be a police officer. I always joke that if I exit, I'll go and be a cop in the Bahamas or something, but that wouldn't stop it from being work. You don't have to love the work; you must love the opportunities it provides and hate the alternative.

Be the person your family can rely on. I'm very passionate about keeping the family together. I told my parents that I want to be the executor of their estate. I would never take anything from them, and I saw what happened after my grandparents died. It was total pandemonium. Everyone was trying to get anything they could get their hands on. It was shameful. I want to be the one who keeps everyone in line when that happens. I am a CEO at work and a CEO in my family.

FEAR FACTOR

If you know where you want to go and you also know what scares you, you can have what scares you push you towards what you want.

JORDAN PETERSON

Focus on what your life would look like if you didn't do the things necessary to accomplish your goals. If your goal is to get in shape, you know you have to go to the gym and eat decently to meet that goal. You should have enough insight to realize that not going to the gym and eating like shit will predispose you to obesity and disease. This is where the alternative drivers come into play. Let the fear of illness and the possibility of your life being cut short drive you to the gym. Even starving rats run away from cheese if they sense a cat.

If you care about a specific cause, allow your love for your motivation to drive you toward the generation of income. You can't give back to your family, community, or cause without money. Advocacy alone can get you only so far without tangible contributions. Love what you can do with money. Help your family, build a new church, save the icebergs, run a nonprofit, or stop global warming. But first, make money to do it.

Most people in the US don't have $6,500 to cough up in an emergency. If you don't have that right now, don't get depressed and anxious about it; make a plan to get it. Fear of being broke should drive you. Fear of not being able to take care of yourself should drive you. Fear of not being in control should drive you. Fear of reliance on others should drive you.

All these forces and more are driving you, pushing you forward. So . . . take the journey. Take the risk. Make the leap. If where you are isn't cutting it, if it's not getting you closer to your goals an inch or a mile at a time, then do something different! Doing more of the same will only give you more of the same!

If I had done "more of the same" when I was starting out, I would have settled into a salaried career as a cop just like my father and grandfather. I would have settled into a builder-grade row house just like everyone I grew up with. I would have settled into . . . life. I would have *settled*.

There isn't anything "wrong" with those things, but that's not the vision I had in my head. It wasn't the life I wanted to choose, so I chose something different. And that choice required me to *do* something different—so, that's what I did. And it's what you have to choose to do if you want to escape the life you *don't* want and run toward the life you *do*.

I did it.

I'm still doing it.

Now, it's your turn.

NOTES

1 Georgia McIntyre, "What Percentage of Small Businesses Fail? (and Other Need-to-Know Stats)," Fundera by NerdWallet, November 20, 2020, https://www.fundera.com/blog/what-percentage-of-small-businesses-fail.

2 "The State of Small Business Now," U.S. Chamber of Commerce, September 16, 2021, https://www.uschamber.com/small-business/state-of-small-business-now.